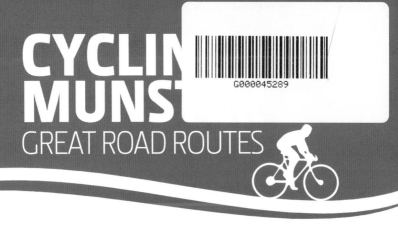

CYCLIN
MUNST
GREAT ROAD ROUTES

Dan MacCarthy, from Skibbereen, County Cork, is a journalist with the *Irish Examiner*. He has had a long-standing interest in the outdoors, which stretches from a childhood spent sailing at Sherkin Island to trekking in Europe and beyond. He is a regular at the Ballyhoura Mountain bike trails and has cycled in England and France, including cycling up the Col du Tourmalet on a mountain bike. He has travelled extensively and lived in Madrid, London and The Hague.

For videos of some of the routes in this guide, photos, other cycling routes at home and abroad, cycling articles and more, visit: www.cyclemunster.com

The Healy Pass

Cycling is a risk sport. The author and The Collins Press accept no responsibility for any injury, loss or inconvenience sustained by anyone using this guidebook.

To the memory of my parents,
Florence and Dan

The author above Lough Derg, County Clare

CYCLING
MUNSTER
GREAT ROAD ROUTES

The Collins Press

First published in 2016 by
The Collins Press
West Link Park
Doughcloyne
Wilton
Cork
T12 N5EF

© Dan MacCarthy 2016

Photos © Dan MacCarthy except for those on pp 37, 38, 103 and 131
which are © Paula Elmore

Dan MacCarthy has asserted his moral right to be identified as the author of this
work in accordance with the Irish Copyright and Related Rights Act 2000.

All rights reserved.

The material in this publication is protected by copyright law. Except as may be
permitted by law, no part of the material may be reproduced (including by storage
in a retrieval system) or transmitted in any form or by any means, adapted, rented
or lent without the written permission of the copyright owners. Applications for
permissions should be addressed to the publisher.

A CIP record for this book is available from the British Library.

Paperback ISBN: 978-1-84889-262-0
PDF eBook ISBN: 978-1-84889-563-8
EPUB eBook ISBN: 978-1-84889-564-5
Kindle ISBN: 978-1-84889-565-2

Design and typesetting by Fairways Design
Typeset in Myriad Pro
Printed in Poland by Białostockie Zakłady Graficzne SA

P. 143: excerpt from 'A Small Farm' by Michael Hartnett from *Collected Poems* (2001)
by kind permission of The Gallery Press and the Estate of Michael Hartnett.

Contents

Routes

Acknowledgements

For the cycling, thanks to my soccer teammates Noel Hayes, Ray O'Reagan, Fabrice Fortune, and Una and Conor O'Mahoney. We struggled on many a daunting hill but enjoyed the thrills of the downhill surges – Up the Column! To Eoin O'Sullivan for accompanying me on the Ring of Kerry, a cycle that proved very doable in the end. For narrowing down the routes and suggesting new ones, Ger Downing and Imelda McSweeney.

For proofreading the script and providing valuable insight: Rory Kelleher, Dan Collins, Flor MacCarthy and Sam Boland. For help with the maps: Dermot Ahern, Brendan Cotter and Ben Howard of Viewranger. com. The maps themselves were adapted from the routes recorded on mapmyride.com. For fact-checking, Pat Walsh. To my brothers Barry and Gerry MacCarthy for buying much-needed equipment for the 5,000km of routes cycled for research. To the Bishopstown Hillwalkers, especially Ellen Ring, for constant advice. To Mark Evans of the *Irish Examiner* for website ideas.

For unfailing encouragement, my sister Clare MacCarthy. To my publisher The Collins Press for having bottomless patience. To all those out on the road who helped me with a lift back to my car after a puncture, or with a glass of water, or for providing direction in seemingly hopeless circumstances. Thanks to Cillian, Jerry and Eoin at the Bike Shed in Dennehy's Cross, Cork, for excellent repairs and service to my bike, often at short notice.

Thanks to all those who agreed to be photographed for the book: John Tynan; Sue O'Connor; MacDonaghs, father and son; Fabrice Fortune; Ray O'Reagan; Deirdre and Jack O'Shea; Brian Keane and Pat Clancy; Jim Fitzgibbon; Simon and Valerie; Hans; Colm and Hugh Murphy; Eamonn McSweeney, Shane Boyd, Ian Cummins, Declan Rennick, and Aidan and Eoin Linehan; Liam English; Skip and Eileen Koblentz; Nicholas Faulkner, Marisa and Marie; Johann; Diane Grislin and Pascal Carre; Vadim and Emils; Emmanuel Ceragioli; Michael Deasy.

Memory is a cruel master so humble apologies to anyone who has helped me in the production of this cycling guide but who isn't named here.

Route Location Map

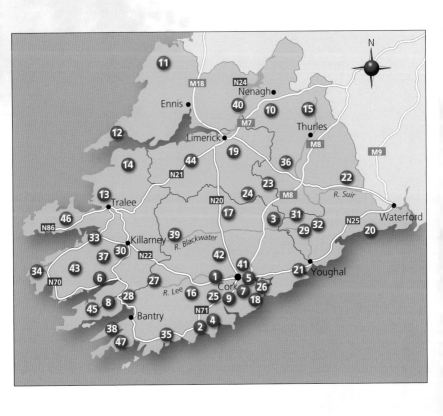

Quick-Reference Route Table

No.	Route	Grade	Range
1	Carrigrohane–Coachford Loop, Cork	2	Short
2	Clonakilty–Inchydoney Return, Cork	2/3	Short
3	Kilworth Circuit, Cork	3	Short
4	Clonakilty–Courtmacsherry Circuit	2/3	Mid
5	Loop East of Cork City	3	Mid
6	Kenmare–Sneem Circuit, Kerry	2	Mid
7	Cork City to Crosshaven Return	2	Mid
8	Adrigole Circuit, Cork & Kerry	3	Mid
9	Cork–Kinsale Loop	3	Mid
10	Silvermines Circuit, Tipperary	3	Mid
11	Lisdoonvarna–Ballyvaughan Return	4/5	Mid
12	Loop Head Peninsula Circuit, Clare	2/3	Mid
13	Blennerville–Ballyheigue Return, Kerry	3/4	Mid
14	Abbeyfeale to the Coast Loop	4	Mid
15	Circuit of North Tipperary	3/4	Mid
16	Gearagh Circuit , Cork	3	Mid
17	Doneraile Figure of Eight, Cork & Limerick	3	Mid
18	Cork–Robert's Cove Return	3	Mid
19	Kilmallock–Caherconlish Circuit	3/4	Mid
20	Copper Coast Loop, Waterford	3/4	Mid
21	Castlemartyr–Youghal Return, Cork	3	Mid
22	South-East Tipperary Circuit	3	Mid
23	Glen of Aherlow Loop, Tipperary	2	Mid
24	Kildorrery–Galbally Figure of Eight	3	Mid
25	Kinsale–Kilmurry Return, Cork	3/4	Mid
26	Cork City–Cobh Return	2	Mid
27	Ballyvourney–Kealkill Loop, Cork & Kerry	4/5	Mid
28	Cork/Kerry Circuit: Coomholla–Kilgarvan	4/5	Mid
29	Youghal and River Blackwater Circuit	3	Mid
30	Ross Castle–Black Valley Loop, Kerry	3	Mid
31	Grand Vee Circuit, Waterford	4/5	Mid
32	Comeraghs Circuit, Waterford	4	Mid
33	Glenbeigh–Caragh Lake Return, Kerry	2	Mid
34	Cahersiveen–Valentia Circuit, Kerry	4	Mid
35	Glandore–Baltimore Loop, Cork	4	Mid
36	Cashel Circuit, Tipperary	3	Mid
37	Circuit of the Reeks, Kerry	4	Mid
38	Sheep's Head Peninsula Loop	3	Mid
39	Millstreet–Gneevgullia Return, Cork	3	Mid
40	East Clare Circuit	2	Mid
41	Loop North from Cork City	4/5	Long
42	Carrigrohane–Kanturk Return, Cork	5	Long
43	Ring of Kerry Challenge	5	Long
44	Charleville to the Coast Loop	5	Long
45	Beara Peninsula Circuit	5	Long
46	Dingle Peninsula Circuit	5	Long
47	Mizen Peninsula Circuit	5	Long

Distance	Ascent	Time	Page
39km	363m	2 to 2.5 hours	18
22km	230m	1 to 1.5 hours	21
38km	601m	2 to 2.5 hours	24
55km	192m	3 to 3.5 hours	27
48km	503m	2.5 to 3 hours	30
58km	675m	3 to 3.5 hours	33
52km	472m	2.5 to 3 hours	36
54km	683m	3 to 3.5 hours	40
65km	993m	3 to 3.5 hours	43
70km	709m	3 to 3.5 hours	46
89km	948m	5 to 5.5 hours	48
61km	475m	3 to 3.5 hours	51
71km	392m	3 to 4 hours	54
92km	596m	4 to 5 hours	57
82km	530m	4 to 4.5 hours	60
66km	306m	3 to 3.5 hours	63
64km	690m	3 to 3.5 hours	66
58km	784m	3 to 3.5 hours	68
86km	570m	4 to 5 hours	70
73km	893m	3 to 4 hours	73
62km	530m	2.5 to 3 hours	76
76km	640m	4 to 4.5 hours	79
47km	507m	2 to 2.5 hours	82
71km	673m	3 to 3.5 hours	85
77km	1,055m	4 to 4.5 hours	88
50km	458m	2.5 to 3 hours	91
86km	1,374m	4.5 to 5.5 hours	94
56km	1,202m	2.5 to 3.5 hours	97
50km	608m	2.5 to 3 hours	99
60km	757m	3 to 3.5 hours	102
94km	1,079m	5 to 6 hours	105
70km	1,092m	4 to 5 hours	108
50km	516m	2.5 to 3 hours	110
66km	824m	4 hours	112
83km	1,050m	5 to 6 hours	115
65km	429m	3 to 3.5 hours	118
86km	1,198m	5 to 6 hours	121
67km	751m	3 to 3.5 hours	124
48km	569m	3 to 3.5 hours	127
45km	293m	2 to 3 hours	130
106km	1,142m	4.5 to 5.5 hours	133
104km	919m	5 to 6 hours	136
171km	1,759m	7 to 10 hours	138
112km	621m	5.5 to 6.5 hours	141
149km	1,998m	7 to 9 hours	144
126km	1,631m	6.5 to 7.5 hours	147
106km	1,347m	6 to 7.5 hours	150

On the Clogheen-to-Lismore road, County Waterford

Introduction

The country appears to have gone completely mad for cycling. You can't stick your head out the window these days without seeing a couple of Lycra-clad cyclists whizzing past. The bike-to-work scheme has been the chief motivator behind the rush in huge numbers of people mounting up. In 2014 the number of cars sold in Ireland was 92,000. The number of bikes sold was 95,000. Long may it continue!

The history of cycling in Ireland is as old as the history of the bike itself. The success of Sean Kelly and Stephen Roche in the 1980s and 1990s and latterly Nicolas Roche and Dan Martin have inspired many people to invest in expensive, professional-standard bikes to contest races at home and abroad. However, for every professional rider there are probably 20,000 leisure cyclists. Many take to the increasing number of greenways which are springing up around the country. The flagship greenway is the Great Western Greenway in County Mayo, which receives 180,000 to 200,000 visitors per year and follows a majestic trail from Westport to Achill Island. Other trails are opening up: Dungarvan, Abbeyfeale, even Dublin to Galway has been mostly built. Cork to Kinsale is promised and Glenbeigh to Cahersiveen in County Kerry promises to be a magnificent track along the old railway carved into the side of the mountains on the Iveragh Peninsula. However, there are a lot more quiet, country roads out there crying out to be explored. Many of them are in pretty decent shape.

Ireland has more kilometres of roadway per person than any other European country. This is probably due to the fragmented nature of our landholdings where, of necessity, lanes and other routes were needed to connect farms to villages and towns. This guide covers a fraction of the estimated 12,000km of roads in Munster. It aims to cover the entire province but, of course, there are areas not covered, as not every road could be included. Some of the routes are clockwise and some anticlockwise. The directions are nearly all chosen in order to have minimal climbing after long distances: very few people would want to take on a climb of 2km with a 10 per cent gradient after cycling 115km.

Happy Cycling!

Using this book

Grading

The gradients are categorised as follows:

1. The easiest graded mountain or hill cycle – short, gentle climbs.
2. Lower gradients, but distances can still be long.
3. Middle-ranking mountain challenge.
4. Very steep hills over short distances or steep climbs over long distances.
5. The most difficult routes, with very steep gradients.

The gradient is calculated by the height gained, divided by the distance travelled, multiplied by 100. A height gain of 100m say, over a 2km (2,000m) climb multiplied by 100 equals a gradient of 5 per cent. $100 \div 2,000 = 0.05$ x $100 = 5$ per cent. Cycling downhill is said to have a negative gradient.

The routes are grouped by range: the first three are short (0–39km); the next 38 are mid-range (40–99km); and the final six are long (100km+). Some of the shorter routes can be tougher than longer ones. An example is the 38km route near Kilworth, which I have graded 3 as it has a long, tough climb and an overall height gain of 601m, compared to, say, the Clonakilty–Courtmacsherry circuit, which climbs 192m over 55km and is, in fact, easier.

Generally speaking, the lower the distance, the easier the cycle but keep a close eye on the height gain and the distribution of the hills in the elevation chart to make sure you are capable of cycling the route. If you are not a regular cyclist it is probably advisable to tackle the mid-range cycles before attempting the very long charity cycles such as the Ring of Kerry.

The routes were, for this writer at least, a voyage of discovery of Munster. Many of the villages were new to me and there was a great thrill in linking up places that I had previously only tenuously connected. The views are simply magnificent. The six major peninsulas that thrust out into the Atlantic in the south-west offer unrivalled cycling and jaw-dropping views. However, to cycle here alone would be to neglect the airy mountains of Tipperary, the breezy coast of Waterford, the dissolving Burren in County Clare and the rural pleasures of Limerick.

Some of these routes cross through remote mountainous areas so be aware that mobile phone coverage may be absent. You are advised not to cycle alone but, if you do, always tell someone your route and expected time of return. It is my experience that in asking for directions you should be equipped with at least a vague idea of where you intend to go. Quite often, locals will not know the name of the road that you are on, but you have checked it and know it's right. They may be oblivious to the hinterland of a given area but don't like to admit it. And they can send you in the wrong direction, so carefully weigh up the advice you are given.

The map scale is provided and differs from map to map. Each map has a compass symbol for orientation. Main towns, villages, rivers, mountains, and national roads are given. Minor roads are not named so cross-reference with the text for exact descriptions of the road you need. The start/finish points are marked, and the routes are all loop cycles. Directional arrows are provided to point out the right route in case of confusion. The elevation bar is an exact reproduction of the elevation of the route and gives an easy-to-read picture of the number of hills involved.

Finally, each time I arrived in a town or village I would reward myself with a refrain from W. B. Yeats' poem 'Sailing to Byzantium'. 'And so I have crossed the seas and come, to the holy city of Kilgarvan' nearly has the same ring to it as the great poet's lines.

Equipment

Almost as important as the bike is the pump. Don't leave home without one. If you are particularly nifty at fixing a puncture on a deserted mountain road in driving rain, then go for it. Otherwise carry a couple of spare tubes. With practice, you can fit these quickly and be on your way within five minutes of getting a puncture.

There is no shortage of high-visibility clothing for cyclists available. You don't have to look like you have been dipped in a can of fluorescent paint: just wear some bright gear. A helmet is vitally important. At the time of writing they are not compulsory but this will probably change.

Clip-in cycling shoes are becoming more popular and you don't have to have a racer to use them. Pedals on hybrids can be changed to racing pedals. Racing tyres, too, can be fitted to hybrid bikes. They are dearer but make a huge difference in cycling long distances.

Gloves are a vital piece of equipment in the colder months. Some people favour the fingerless variety but these or the full-glove variety are essential when it is cold. They are also useful year-round as they prevent chafing, blistering and calluses.

A visor to keep flies out of your eyes is a good idea.

For longer cycles, padded Lycra shorts or leggings will really save your posterior. And make sure your saddle is a good fit. Consider attaching a gel saddle for more comfort.

It is great fun to record your route, or check pre-loaded maps for directions. There are a variety of apps for your smartphone enabling you to do this: mapmyride.com; strava.com; viewranger.com. Most bike shops have holders that fit easily onto handlebars with a see-through, touch-friendly window to see the phone.

Safety

Make sure your bike is in a roadworthy condition. You don't want it to fall apart in traffic or when you're flying down a hill. Bring it for a service to your bike shop if unsure.

Cycle on the left and keep in tight to the margins. Try not to wander into the middle of the road. However, you and another cyclist are legally entitled to cycle two abreast. Single file if overtaking.

Always look behind when starting, crossing lanes or turning.

Always indicate, especially, leaving roundabouts. Fling your arm out at a right angle to indicate where you intend going. Cyclists are often targets for vitriol for disobeying the rules of the road, so don't give drivers reason to hurl abuse at you.

Bring your lights, back and front, if there's a possibility you may return at dusk (or dawn).

Don't forget your lock, as your bike may be unattended for a period.

Wear a helmet.

Headphones: leave them at home. You need to hear what's going on around you.

Climate

Irish weather is notoriously unpredictable. It is a good idea to bring a small knapsack with raingear. There are light, back-hugging knapsacks available.

Sunglasses or a visor are very important for sunny days, even in winter when the sun low in the sky can be blinding.

Many Irish roads are low-lying, coastal or inland, and are prone to flooding. Check the forecast and cross-check with your route to see if there's a risk along your itinerary.

Contacts

Emergency Services: For all emergencies dial 999. This includes gardaí, ambulance, fire brigade, mountain rescue, coastguard. You can also dial the EU number 112, which connects to the same services. This number can be dialled in all EU countries. Both numbers are free of charge.

Weather Forecast: for weather forecasts, check the Met Éireann website (met.ie) or www.mountain-forecast.com. The accuweather.com app also provides good information.

National Parks: Several national parks are encountered along these routes. The Lisdoonvarna–Ballyvaughan route passes through the Burren: www.burrennationalpark.ie. Some of the Kerry routes pass in or near the Killarney National Park which is a joy to explore: www.killarneynationalpark.ie. On the Ballyvourney–Kealkil route, Gougane Barra park is passed – not a national park but still worth a visit: www.gouganebarra.com.

Websites

There are over 400 cycling clubs with 26,000 members in Ireland affiliated to www.cyclingireland.ie.

Other useful and interesting websites are:
www.boards.ie/cycling
www.womenscycling.ie
www.trackcycling.ie
www.trailbadger.com
www.irishcycling.com
https://cyclist.ie
www.stickybottle.com

1. Carrigrohane–Coachford Loop, Cork

Carrigrohane – Coachford – Ballincollig – Carrigrohane

Location:	County Cork
Grade:	2
Distance:	39km
Height gain:	363m
Duration:	2 to 2.5 hours
Verdict:	Nice rural cycle with unexpected views

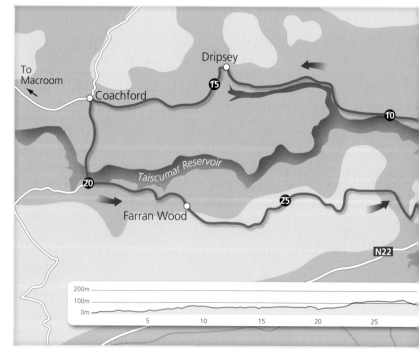

Start/finish

The start point is the Angler's Rest pub in Carrigrohane. To reach it, drive 4km west out of Cork city on the N22/Carrigrohane Road and turn right onto the R618. The Angler's Rest is just north of the River Lee, with a car park on the opposite side of the road.

Cycling above Inniscarra Dam, Cork

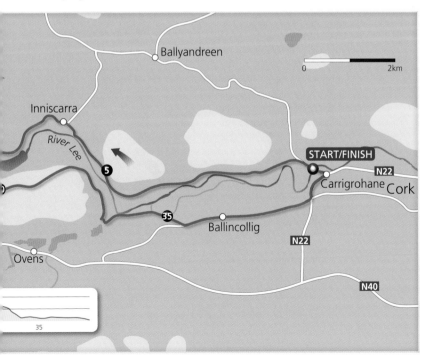

19

The outbound section of this route is very popular with cyclists; drivers mainly allow a lot of space. Views of the River Lee as it courses along are frequently afforded over the ditches and through the trees.

Route description

Cycle westwards on the R618/Inniscarra Road and at a busy junction take the left option to stay on this road. The area is heavily wooded and a green canopy of native trees envelops the road for several kilometres. The road virtually follows the river curve by curve till it reaches the Inniscarra Dam after 8km. The hydroelectric dam was opened in 1956 to provide electricity, mainly to the city. It provided huge employment for labourers and suppliers once construction got under way. However, it dramatically changed the landscape. One downside was the loss of ancient monuments sunk forever beneath the rising tide. These include Castle Inch on the southern side of the river and the sixth-century Innislinga Abbey, founded by St Senan. Today, the Inniscarra Dam is also an important fishery, with tench, rudd and carp prominent.

Continue to the hamlet of Dripsey on the R618 and cross a lovely old bridge on the River Dripsey, which is a tributary of the Lee. The village of Coachford lies another 4km along the road. Turn south here onto the R619 and continue across the reservoir. Once across, turn right onto the L2202. This road passes by the predominantly coniferous forest of Farran Wood, which is very popular with walkers. The road is roughly parallel to the south bank of the reservoir, about 1km away across the fields.

At the first obvious crossroads bear left. This road will connect to the main Cork-to-Killarney road, the N22, which no cyclist in his/her right mind would want to take. Instead, take a sharp left just before the road descends. This narrow road is very popular with cyclists and walkers. It is a haven of peace on the doorstep of the city and there are great views of the Inniscarra Dam. Continue for 3km due east before the road turns south for 1km and then east again through a wood till intersecting the R608 which runs through Ballincollig to Cork. Continue to the end of the town and go left at the roundabout and then left at the next traffic lights. The start/finish point is 200m ahead.

2. Clonakilty– Inchydoney Return, Cork

Clonakilty – Inchydoney – Dunmore House – Clonakilty

Location:	County Cork
Grade:	2/3
Distance:	22km
Height gain:	230m
Duration:	1 to 1.5 hours
Verdict:	Abundance of nature; a few tough hills

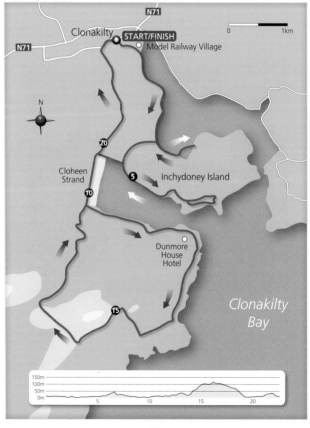

Start/finish

From Cork city, take the N71 to Clonakilty. Park at the car park on Casement Street on the bypass road to Skibbereen. Retrace your drive 400m for the road to Inchydoney.

This starts out as a carefree, relaxing cycle along the fringes of the Clonakilty wetlands and is ideal for families or occasional cyclists. Though it is a short cycle, it is not necessarily an easy one. Beginners are recommended to turn back at Dunmore House Hotel as there are some tough hills thereafter. Also, on the approach to Inchydoney, there is a hilly climb on the one-way system both in and out, so it may be an idea to wheel the bike both ways on the lower road.

Cycling along Clonakilty Bay

Route description

Follow the Inchydoney road south, past the Model Railway Village, which is ever popular with junior train drivers. Almost immediately, the waters of Clonakilty Bay come into view: a vast network of open water, lagoons and mudflats. Several causeways allow passage across the wetlands. After a gentle 2km cycle and a passage across the first causeway, the road reaches a T-Junction. While the left turn ends in a cul-de-sac it is worth taking for the views back across the bay from the second causeway on the route. Grey herons and egrets frequent the reeds on the right of this causeway. At low tide in late spring and autumn especially, a mass of green algal bloom gives a lustrous sheen, if not a challenging stink, to the entire bay while at high tide the waters lap the low wall.

Once back at the T-junction, continue straight and ignore the right turn after 1km. The inner area is known as the Cloheen Strand and is described by the National Parks and Wildlife Service as having a 'fine range of habitats from saline lagoons, to brackish grasslands, open freshwater marsh and wet grassland'. With its numerous herds of horses grazing at the water's edge it resembles the famed Camargue wetland of southern France.

The region is a Special Protection Area under the EU Birds Directive of special conservation interest for shelduck, dunlin, black-tailed godwit and curlew. It is known to have several species of vagrant American birds as well as rare sightings of black-winged stilt, long-billed dowitcher and lesser yellowlegs.

Continue along the seafront to Inchydoney. At low tide this is a giant mudflat with hundreds of birds of several different species alighting and foraging. Entering Inchydoney, incoming traffic is directed to the left. The hotel is a good spot for a break if needed. Leave the former island by the same route but this time take the first road to the left, which we passed earlier.

This road skirts the southern part of the bay and leads to Dunmore House Hotel. Continue past the hotel. The road has two 90-degree turns (right, then left) before arriving at a crossroads. Go right for 1km, climbing a steep hill. A super descent for 2km returns the rider to a point passed earlier at the corner of the bay. Skirt the bay again and go straight through the next junction. This hilly road leads back to Clonakilty after 2km. The start/finish point is a little to the right.

3. Kilworth Circuit, Cork

Kilworth – Araglin – Ballyporeen – Kilworth

Location:	County Cork
Grade:	3
Distance:	38km
Height gain:	601m
Duration:	2 to 2.5 hours
Verdict:	Pastoral beauty but tough climbs

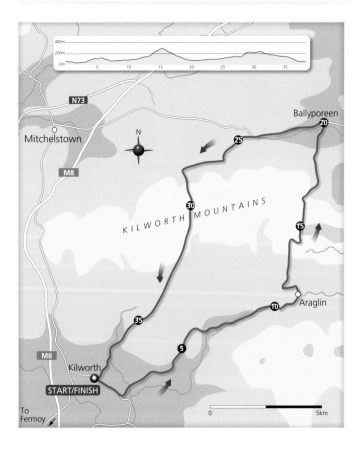

Start/finish

Start in the pleasant village of Kilworth a few kilometres north-east of Fermoy. To reach it, exit off the M8 at Junction 14 onto the R639.

The road from Araglin, County Cork, to Ballyporeen, County Tipperary, with the Galtees in the background

Appearances can be deceptive. There are 601m of climbing in just 38km in this route, which follows a meandering roll along relatively flat ground for the first 10km. Thus, the route should be categorised as difficult even though the distance suggests it is none too onerous. The western flank of the Knockmealdowns is the culprit for the harder task.

As you approach the village from Fermoy keep an eye out over the treetops for the Norman Cloghleagh Castle. This was the site in 1643 of a massacre of twenty of castle owner Richard Condon's family by English forces under Charles Vavasour. His forces in turn were slaughtered the next day in an ambush by the Irish army.

Route description

Suitably chastened, take the R667 in the direction of Lismore and branch off to the left (north) after 1km. The next 10km stretch is a wonderful, peaceful cycle on quiet country roads through a wood for the most part. The River Araglin, a Blackwater tributary, gurgles softly below the road to the left. Approaching Araglin, sheep can be glimpsed through the beech trees grazing on the banks of the river in a pastoral scene straight out of William Wordsworth. The name Araglin evokes glories of a bygone era or some lordly intrigue. Alas, the hamlet appears to have fallen on hard times with the closure of a pub and other buildings and has lost some of its former magic.

Once in Araglin, about-turn and take the second right, which rises to the right and curves away. After 1km take a sharp right and begin a long climb to the summit. The start point (the right-hand turn) is at 100m and the top of the road is at 300m, 4km away. Most of it is an 11 per cent gradient. This is the road that makes it a much harder cycle than the others in the short category. In fact, it is ideal training for the Ring of Kerry cycle. In addition, the road quality is poor (but not terrible). Glance back to see the Araglin Valley spread out in all its verdant splendour. Just ahead, the formidable Galtees beckon as the road plunges and dives past hedgerows, barking dogs, farmhouses and toppling wild rose bushes before fetching up in the famous village of Ballyporeen.

In 1984 the village hosted the then US president Ronald Reagan whose visit drew the wrath of over 600 people protesting his foreign policy. Ballyporeen is one of two places in this book to have hosted a US president (Moneygall in Route 15, Circuit of North Tipperary, being the other). The village has a fine, spacious boulevard, unlike most villages. Go left on the R665 in the direction of Mitchelstown but branch off to the left after 3km. (Don't take the road on the extreme left.) After 4km the road turns 90 degrees to the south (left) and a very pleasant 10km cycle returns the rider to Kilworth.

4. Clonakilty–Courtmacsherry Circuit

Clonakilty – Old Chapel – Timoleague – Courtmacsherry – Clonakilty

Location:	County Cork
Grade:	2/3
Distance:	55km
Height gain:	192m
Duration:	3 to 3.5 hours.
Verdict:	Semi-coastal route. Attractive villages.

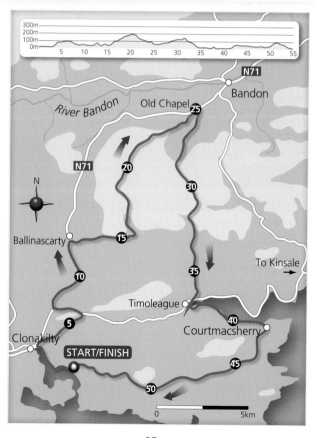

Start/finish

From Cork city, take the N71 to Clonakilty. Take the first exit at the roundabout, which splits in two immediately – take the second road along the coast. Follow this road for 3km to Ring. Park at or near the pier.

The seafront at the east side of Courtmacsherry in west Cork

This is a lovely, ambling cycle switching between rolling countryside and coast and visiting two pearls of west Cork: the villages of Timoleague and Courtmacsherry.

Route description

Retrace the route along the bay (great for birdwatching) back into Clonakilty and just before the roundabout turn right and climb the road parallel to the N71 road to Cork. This is the Old Timoleague Road, R600, and is obviously quieter than the main road. After 3km, swing left, where you pick up the N71. It is a very busy road but it is wide. Bear with it for a while and you will shortly be back into leafy surroundings.

The village of Ballinascarty materialises after 3km. This was home to the father of Henry Ford, William, and a fine silver example of a Model T stands proudly by the side of the main road in honour of this major figure of modern industrial history, who built the prototype for the car. Take a right here and another straight away and head due east for 3.5km. At the junction turn left, heading north. This is very attractive countryside and you rise and fall like a cork on the sea as you bob along through the fields and hedgerows.

After 3km there is another junction. This time turn right. This road brings you past some huge houses – excesses of the Celtic Tiger – and some aggressive dogs, if you're unlucky, before arriving at the hamlet of Old Chapel on the outskirts of Bandon. This is almost the halfway point of this fairly leisurely jaunt. Now take a hard right, about 160 degrees, onto the R602 to Timoleague. This road is of fairly reasonable quality with undramatic surroundings. However, after cycling about 4km it descends on a glorious downwards sweep into Timoleague which lasts for 6km. Ahead is the narrow, shallow inlet of Courtmacsherry Bay, famous for wading birds including godwit, curlew, whimbrel and dunlin. The ruined fourteenth-century Franciscan friary at Timoleague is a dramatic presence in the village and is an amazing sight when lit up at night.

Continue along the water's edge on the R601 on an excellent flat road to the mellifluous-sounding village of Courtmacsherry. The name has nothing to do with alcohol, though: it is simply an anglicisation of the Irish *Cúirt Mhic Seafraidh* (MacSherry's Court). In 1915, Courtmacsherry Lifeboat Station sent a rescue boat to aid the stricken RMS *Lusitania*. The road which links the two villages is great for walking, too, with a dedicated path. The village is a good spot for refreshments.

At the end of the village the road turns and climbs right. It passes above Courtmacsherry and through a wooded area, which runs right down to the sea. A small road to a fine beach, Broadstrand, leads off to the left. This area is predominantly farmland with open views to the Atlantic. From here the route is more or less in a straight line, 10km, back to Ring pier and the car, with no confusing forks.

5. Loop East of Cork City

Cork city – Glanmire – Fota Island – Passage West – Cork city

Location:	County Cork
Grade:	3
Distance:	48km
Height gain:	503m
Duration:	2.5 to 3 hours
Verdict:	Interesting mix of city and country cycling

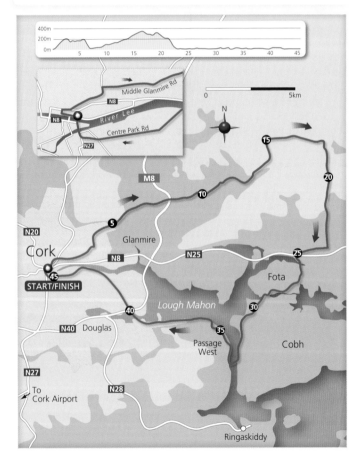

Start/finish

The start point for this route is in Cork city centre. There are several public car parks in the city. Ideally, use the one on St Patrick's Quay, which has a pedestrian exit onto MacCurtain Street. Alternatively, park outside the city centre and cycle in.

The old railway line between Passage West and Riverstown, Cork

This is an ideal cycle for a summer's evening. Plenty of elevation to start with but rewarded by some glorious descents and a satisfying exploration of Cork city's eastern geography. Added bonus of a ferry trip!

Route description

Head east on MacCurtain Street and cycle up the hill to the left at the first junction on Summerhill North/the R614. This is a toughish climb of just under 2km with a 7 per cent gradient at the end. Well, no one ever claimed that Cork was flat!

Halfway up the hill lies the genteel old district of the city – St Luke's – with its quaint Victorian-style kiosk and grand church. The views from here over the city are peerless. Continue up the hill and turn right at the next traffic lights. This is the Old Youghal Road, once the great east–west artery carrying trade and traders into the heart of the city.

31

At the next junction the route briefly intersects the North Ring Road at Mayfield. Go left for 50m after the traffic lights before turning right at the next set of lights and back onto the Old Youghal Road. The road gradually leaves behind the suburbs and the thin industrial belt.

After 1km, a road to the right leads downhill via Church Hill to Glanmire. Skip it and maintain an easy climb before suddenly plunging in the direction of Glanmire. The route now intersects the R639 – the Watergrasshill-to-Glanmire road. Cross through the junction and pick up the L3010 – a straight line from whence you came. There is another brief suburban area to contend with before being enveloped by countryside. The road is pretty straight for the next 5km and passes through some gorgeous woodland. The road swings left and north for 3km before arriving at a junction at Pigeon Hill.

From here, take the road to the extreme right, which continues straight for 3km. Watch out for a road to the right at 90 degrees. Take it, and plunge gloriously downhill for 5km. Ignore the minor junction until reaching a bigger T-junction. Across the road is a small cul-de-sac. Go right for 2km and then hard left at the roundabout in the direction of Cobh. This is the R624 and it skirts Fota Wildlife Park which is home to Sumatran tigers, cheetahs and giraffes, among many exotic species. Cross a small arched bridge and go right towards Cobh.

The cross-river ferry appears just under 4km along and costs €2 per bike. Take the ferry and on disembarking turn right into Passage West. On the outskirts of this village there is a great cycle/walking path just to the right, along the seafront. This is the old Passage West-to-Cork railway line and goes to the heart of the city exclusively on an off-road track bar a 1km section from Hop Island onwards. At the Rochestown Inn the cycle track is to the right, next to an apartment block. Continue to Cork city either by cycling straight ahead or going right just after the old red railway bridge.

6. Kenmare–Sneem Circuit, Kerry

Kenmare – Sneem – Moll's Gap – Kenmare

Location:	County Kerry
Grade:	2
Distance:	58km
Height gain:	675m
Duration:	3 to 3.5 hours
Verdict:	Short but very sweet exploration of the Iveragh Peninsula

Start/finish

Kenmare, County Kerry. Start on the western side of the town.

This route begins in the inviting town of Kenmare and takes in a section of the Ring of Kerry. For anyone contemplating that route it is worth doing for familiarisation purposes alone. However, while the famous charity cycle route is an anticlockwise expedition, this is a clockwise foray. The section to Sneem mimics the Kerry Way walking route, a 200km circuit of the peninsula.

Route description

From Kenmare, take the N71 towards Killarney but turn left almost immediately onto the N70. This road is of reasonable quality and it lands you in the village of Templenoe after 6km. This heavily wooded area culminates at Blackwater Bridge 5km farther on. The lofty double-arched bridge is almost 200 years old and is a protected heritage structure. The Blackwater River drains the hinterland of Mullaghnattin and Knocklomena mountains. In fact, apart from the roads linking Kenmare to Killarney and Moll's Gap to the Gap of Dunloe, the road inland from this bridge is the only one that crosses the peninsula. The bridge is a useful point to explore inland on other cycle routes, most notably the wonderful Ballaghbeama Pass which lies about 12km north.

Press on to the village of Sneem. Just prior to the village is the Parknasilla Hotel, which has counted among its guests George Bernard Shaw and Princess Grace of Monaco, and used as a location in the Colin Farrell film

The Lobster. It was once owned by Great Southern and Western Railways, which brought guests by steam train from America via Dublin as far as Kenmare and onwards to the hotel by carriage. The hotel is surrounded by a 500-acre estate of native woodland and has many exotic plants. It looks out on an archipelago of small islands, one of which, Illaunslea, was the childhood home of the writer Peter Somerville Large.

The N70 takes a 90-degree turn at Parknasilla before depositing you in Sneem 3km farther on. The Ring of Kerry and the Kerry Way wind their way westward from here. However, this route turns inland at the village square on the R568. Possessing one of the more curious place names in Ireland, Sneem is worthy of explanation: the modern village name is an anglicisation of '*An tSnaidhm*' which translates as 'the Knot' and probably refers to the swirling waters of the River Sneem.

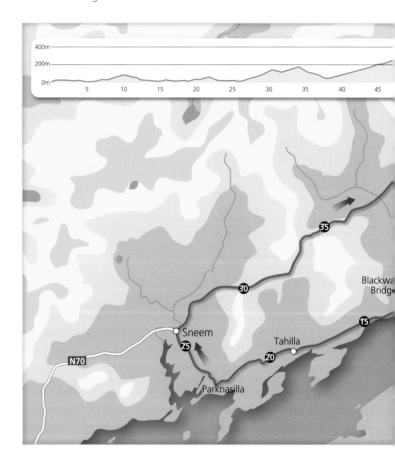

For at least the first 10km of this latter section of the route there are gasp-inducing vistas of Kenmare River (Bay) and the Beara Peninsula opposite. Then comes a decent downhill section of 4km before the road rises to Moll's Gap on an incline that is not too tasking. Just before the gap there is a viewing area of the famous Black Valley and the towering MacGillycuddy's Reeks whose pinnacle, Carrauntoohil, is the tallest mountain in Ireland. Moll's Gap is a popular tourist stop with a large cafe. Left here would take you to Killarney but instead swing right on the N71 and a glorious 9km descent to Kenmare.

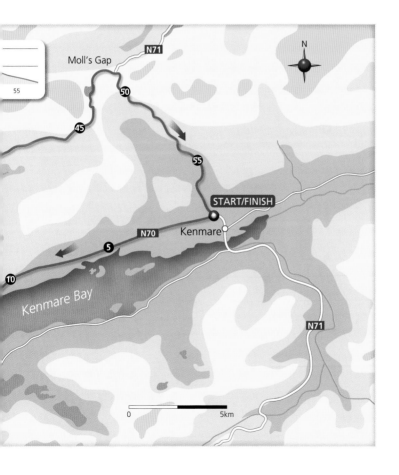

7. Cork City to Crosshaven Return

Cork – Passage West – Crosshaven – Carrigaline – Cork

Location:	County Cork
Grade:	2
Distance:	52km
Height gain:	472m
Duration:	2.5 to 3 hours
Verdict:	Off-road cycling for 50 per cent of the time. Beside the sea.

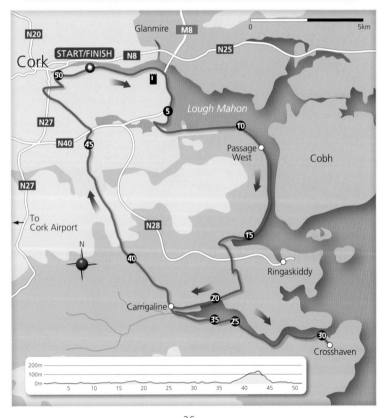

Start/finish

Victoria Road, Cork city centre. There are several public car parks in the city centre. The closest to the start point is City Hall car park.

The track from Carrigaline, County Cork, follows the former railway line

f there is an optimum time for cycling any of the routes in this guide it is probably a summer's evening. This relatively short route can be knocked out in easily under three hours, or slightly longer if you stop along the way.

Route description

Start at the junction of Albert Quay and Victoria Road near the Idle Hour pub. This is frequently a very busy quay as ships unload their cargo – often timber. Look north across the river to the suburbs of Montenotte and Tivoli – named after towns in Italy. It is not possible to cycle along the river as there are several commercial premises. Instead, cycle to the end of Victoria Road and take the first left onto the leafy Centre Park Road. This road would have boulevard status were it not for the multiple potholes and tree roots that penetrate its surface but there is room for two-way traffic.

The road comes to a T-Junction and the elegant River Lee, which has risen 90km west in the Shehy Mountains on the Cork/Kerry border. At this point it is a languorous river on which you variously see rowers, pleasure craft and commercial shipping. Across the river are the Tivoli Docks with

37

The charming village of Crosshaven, County Cork

giant gantries unloading cargo. Pass Cork's GAA stadium on the right. Páirc Uí Chaoimh, at the time of writing, is undergoing a huge reconstruction.

Very soon the poorly surfaced road brings you to Blackrock pier. Press on to the castle along a better surfaced road past a string of period homes on the right. The castle has undergone many transformations from a private dwelling to its current status as an observatory. From here a lovely meandering public pathway brings you to a T-junction after 4km. Go left. The path is very popular with walkers too, so take care. Go left (not right) at the road junction, past the Rochestown Inn onto the main road, the R610. After 1km cycle to the left and the start of the old Passage West-to-Cork railway which has been converted to a walkway/cycleway. With Lough Mahon on the left proceed to Passage West and join the main road across a small park. Press onwards to Monkstown. Pass the cross-river ferry to Cobh (see Route 5).

Stay on the road till a sharp left brings you above the water. After 1km it intersects the N28. Continue through the junction for 2km and swing right when you meet the R613 at a T-junction. After 2km, take a left at the first traffic lights on the outskirts of Carrigaline. Then take the first exit, left, at the roundabout onto the R612. On the left after 1km is a car park through which one can access a wonderful cycle path on a dedicated track right out to Crosshaven with the wonderfully named Drake's Pool a delightful distraction. Francis Drake is reputed to have sought refuge here from the Spanish Armada in 1589. The track follows the former Passage West-to-Crosshaven railway, which closed in 1932. Cronin's Pub is great for refreshments.

The outward cycle track along by Drake's Pool is too lovely not to take on the way back. Retrace the inward path back to the traffic lights in Carrigaline and go left followed by a right at the next crossroads. Then go left at the next roundabout onto West Avenue. This is a quiet country road that brings you to the suburb of Douglas after 7km – with some toughish climbs. Follow the signs for the city centre along the Douglas Road and turn right on Blackrock Road. Pass the hospital and take a sharp left after 1km onto Victoria Road.

8. Adrigole Circuit, Cork & Kerry

*Adrigole – Castletownbere – Eyeries – Ardgroom
– Lauragh – Adrigole*

Location:	Counties Cork and Kerry
Grade:	3
Distance:	54km
Height gain:	683m
Duration:	3 to 3.5 hours
Verdict:	Superb short cycle on the Beara Peninsula with unrivalled views

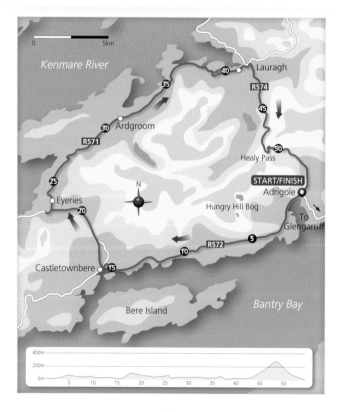

Start/finish

The start point is the village of Adrigole on the Beara Peninsula, on the R572 west of Glengarriff. There are a couple of small car parks on the left at the end of the village.

Cycling above Glanmore Lake on the way to Lauragh, County Kerry, from the Healy Pass on the Cork/Kerrry border

Adrigole is probably one of the longest villages in the country, stretching on for several kilometres. This route takes in views of Hungry Hill, immortalised by Daphne du Maurier in her 1943 novel of the same name, and Castletownbere, a bustling town with much activity around the pier where huge trawlers are tied up. It was also the home of Dr Aidan MacCarthy whose Second World War memoir, *A Doctor's War*, was recently made into a documentary film.

Route description

Leaving Adrigole, with the sea on your left, cycle under the monolithic presence of Hungry Hill, the highest peak in the Caha Range at 685m.

The road hugs the coast until Castletownbere, 15km away. There is a great view of one of the biggest islands in the country, Bere Island. Just before Bere Island is Roancarrig Lighthouse, decommissioned since 2012.

The winding road from Adrigole, County Cork, leading to the Healy Pass

The main road continues to the end of the peninsula but our route goes right on the R571, on the approach to Castletownbere, crossing the Slieve Miskish mountains into the exceptionally colourful village of Eyeries. Why so many of the residents painted their houses in vivid colours like a Bridget Riley painting is a question to be wondered at but not asked. The road to the village is hilly as it leaves Castletownbere and the fine descent on a fairly good road for 5km into the kaleidoscope village is a thrill.

With Kenmare River (Bay) in view now, swing right, still on the R571 with the sea on the left. The roads are very quiet with plenty of solitude for the lone cyclist. There are good views out to sea of Scariff and Deenish islands, neighbours to the much more famous Skelligs. Back on the road and a good surface brings us past the headland of Tuosist from where cyclist Jake Bullough set out in 2008 to cycle to Iran.

Next is the village of Ardgroom, a pleasant spot and fine for a stop. After 4km, you cross the (unmarked) Cork/Kerry border and up along the road is a nice pub at the townland of Lauragh, An Síbín Bar. The area is heavily wooded with lush vegetation all around.

After coffee take the R574 to the right, which leads to the Healy Pass, 9km distant. It is a fairly difficult climb but the thought of the descent on the other side is a great motivator. You mark off 250m in 6km – a 4 per cent gradient. The pass marks the Kerry/Cork border.

Take a rest at the top to take in the dumbfounding views: ahead to Bantry Bay and the Sheep's Head Peninsula, behind to the Iveragh Peninsula and Kenmare River. A stupendous bending road descends to Adrigole and returns you to your car.

9. Cork–Kinsale Loop

Cork – Fivemilebridge – Belgooly – Brownsmills –
Kinsale – Sandycove – Kinsale – Belgooly – Riverstick –
Fivemilebridge – Cork

Location:	County Cork
Grade:	3
Distance:	65km
Height gain:	993m
Duration:	3 to 3.5 hours
Verdict:	Spectacular countryside and a variety of topography, both riverine and coastal

Start/finish

Start 300m from the Kinsale Road roundabout heading towards Cork city on the Kinsale Road. There is a small cycle track on the left with some adjacent parking on the road near the Harvey Norman store.

The industrial outskirts of Cork city contain a hidden treasure in the Tramore River. Prepare to be seduced by the sounds and sights of the countryside in the city. Thereafter, explore some charming villages, see the sea and return enchanted at the discovery of a new route.

Route description

From the start point, join the Tramore River heading west on a nice cycling/walking path through lush vegetation. This joins the Togher Road. Go left and, just up ahead, left again at a mini-roundabout. This climb from Cork to the back airport road is a meanie, no doubt about it. Rising over 100m in 1.5km is steep. But think of the freewheeling ahead! After five minutes' grunting and panting, you will reach the top of Mathew's Hill. This is one of many severe climbs out of, and in, the city.

No other Irish city or town has such murderous or, depending on taste, magnificent hills. There are at least forty such exits or entrances to the city, north and south – west being the valley of the meandering River Lee and east, the harbour.

Careering past the back of the airport with its antennae, wind socks and plane spotters avidly searching the sky for the latest jumbo, plunge through a small wood and emerge at the first node: the Fivemilebridge

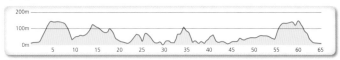

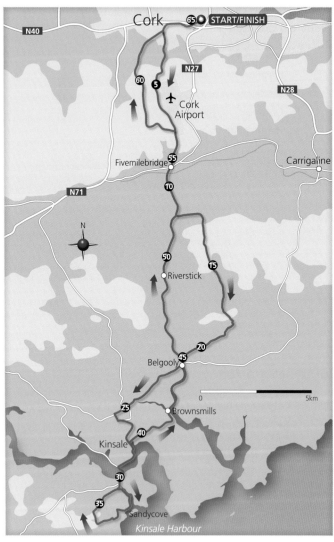

junction. It is a very busy road so exercise caution. Onwards on the R600 towards Kinsale, cycling on the recently built stretch of road, take a sharp left after 2.5km onto very quiet roads. A sharp right, followed by a tough climb and Belgooly is just up the road.

Approaching Kinsale from Belgooly

Arrive at the next crossroads and yet again there is no signpost to help on the way. A murder of crows screeching in the ash trees is the only sign of life. Soon help is at hand as a car door closes behind a wall of trees and a local man says, yes indeed, this is the road to Belgooly.

Speed into the village and turn right towards Brownsmills past the River Stick (hence the name of the village upriver) and continue up a medium hill past a grand farm entrance on the left. A striking set of pillars leads into rolling hills with mature horse chestnuts on the hilltop, straight out of a Thomas Hardy novel. A second tributary of the River Stick flows through Brownsmills. When I climbed from Brownsmills, I spotted a pair of courting kingfishers in the tree branches.

Very quiet roads lead to the outskirts of tourist hotspot Kinsale, gourmet capital of Ireland, where soon there is a great dive through the approaching hills and on through the town, which is magnificently sited on the River Bandon estuary. The town, with its quaint antique shops and bijou art galleries, again calls to mind a nineteenth-century English novel: this time *The Old Curiosity Shop* by Dickens.

Continue on to the beautiful road to the west of the town, which winds along by the yachts to a bridge spanning the River Bandon. Across the bridge take a sharp left, followed by a sharp right and follow the signs to Sandycove and a well-deserved picnic after 34km, at a spot overlooking Sandycove Island.

The route home goes back to Kinsale. Then follow the main road back to Cork but turn off left 1.5km after Fivemilebridge. There is a brief, tough climb for 1.5km, followed by a right-hand turn at a T-junction, and then a glorious descent home via Spur Hill and the Togher Road. The views of the city from this elevation alone are worth the trip.

10. Silvermines Circuit, Tipperary

Nenagh – Silvermines – Newport – Inch – Dolla – Nenagh

Location:	County Tipperary
Grade:	3
Distance:	70km
Height gain:	709m
Duration:	3 to 3.5 hours
Verdict:	Fine rural cycle on the country roads of north-west Tipperary

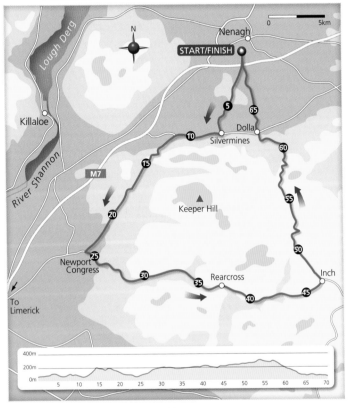

Start/finish

Park to the west of Nenagh near the road to Limerick. The desired road is the R497 to Dolla.

Tranquility abounds on this beautiful cycle through north Tipperary, which visits Silvermines. This enchanting name, unsurprisingly, relates to deposits of silver in the mountains, from which a profitable industry developed over several centuries. Later on, seams of zinc, lead, copper and baryte were found. However, Silvermines is a grand name and very evocative. Barytemines doesn't have the same ring.

Route description

Take the R497 heading towards Dolla. This gentle, easy road forks after 2km. Go right, to the village of Silvermines, which is nestled at the foot of the Silvermine Mountains.

At the village, turn right onto the R499 and continue on good roads for 4km to a junction. Go left in the direction of Killoscully, on the L2110. The RTÉ drama *Killinaskully* was filmed here. This is the vicinity of the highest mountain in the area, Keeper Hill. Several (rival!) bike routes are marked out. In fact, this entire cycle describes a wide circle of the mountain of which great views are now afforded.

Continue along this road in a south-westerly direction. The road is sometimes reasonable and occasionally very poor. The road cuts through woods and crosses several rivers before coming to the very busy town of Newport. This is a good spot for a break as there are a couple of fine pubs.

Now take a sharp left onto the R503 in the direction of Inch, 25km distant. Apart from a minor climb at the start, this is largely a road with a good surface and for most of the 25km has a downhill gradient, allowing for a great speed to be built up. With the Slieve Felim Mountains on the right, you come to the village of Rearcross. It has a peculiar-looking church with walls of corrugated tin, which was built for the Wesleyan community in Northumbria but dismantled and brought to Rearcross in the 1880s. Continue straight through the village. At Inch, take a sharp left and turn due north on the R497. The great Irish singer Shane MacGowan of The Pogues was born at nearby Upperchurch.

This is another fine mountainous road and passes the eastern flank of the Silvermines. Pass a sign for Keeper's Hill (NB: that route is only suitable for mountain bikes). Just after the village of Curreeny is a picnic spot which offers yet more superb views of the Silvermines. Dolla is the final nexus on the road home. Turn left at the Eagle's Nest Bar for 100m before a right-hand turn that will bring you back to the car after 10km. On the right, the River Nenagh flows to the town, which is one of the few examples in the country of a town and river having the same name.

11. Lisdoonvarna–Ballyvaughan Return

Lisdoonvarna – Doolin – Liscannor – Lahinch – Ennistymon –
Kilfenora – Ballyvaughan – Fanore – Lisdoonvarna

Location:	County Clare
Grade:	4/5
Distance:	89km
Height gain:	948m
Duration:	5 to 5.5 hours
Verdict:	Stunning coastal and interior route, with moderate traffic. Good roads and poor roads.

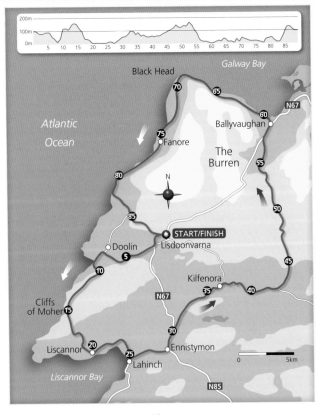

Start/finish

Lisdoonvarna. There is ample car parking in the town centre.

When God made County Clare he was definitely in a good mood. Perhaps second to none in terms of the spectacular in Ireland, the county would seem to have it all: nature, landscape, history in abundance. If something could be done about all the one-off housing you might have a paradise. This route offers spectacular scenery of both a coastal and inland nature. The mix of good and poor roads is more than compensated for by the fantastic views. Note that there is moderate traffic to be expected and take care accordingly.

The Blackhead Lighthouse beside the road from Ballyvaughan, County Clare

Route description

Start in the matchmaking centre of the universe, Lisdoonvarna, popularised by Christy Moore's brilliant song. Cycle south-west on the R478 to Doolin and briefly the R479. The roads around here are busy as you are in the hinterland of the world-famous Cliffs of Moher which tower 215m (700 feet) above the Atlantic. (They are well worth the visit – just follow the signposts.) Arriving at the scattered settlement of Doolin, turn left and follow the coast road for a few kilometres. The Aran Islands can be seen from here. Great for cycling too, but in a different province: Connacht. Pass by the sixteenth-century Doonagore Castle and spare a thought for the 170 Spanish sailors of the Armada who were shipwrecked on the cliffs near the castle in 1588. They were part of a large expeditionary force to help in a putative Irish rebellion and were duly hanged for their trouble.

Very soon on the R478 the entry point atop the Cliffs of Moher appears. A great downhill run takes you to the village of Liscannor and onwards to Lahinch in a matter of minutes. This is as far south as the route goes. Now head east, on the busy N67 (just 4km) to the attractive town of Ennistymon (famed, as are many towns in Clare, for traditional music). Cycle through the town and onwards for a couple of kilometres before veering right onto the R481 to Kilfenora – the inspiration for a great poem by Clare poet Paul Durcan, 'The Kilfenora Teaboy'.

Six kilometres east of the village on the R476, pick up the R480 at a ruined castle and take a sharp left. The road surface leaves a lot to be desired in places here but the scenery gradually becomes spectacular. The blazing grey sheets of the Burren landscape contrast with the vivid green of the fields and the effect is stunning. Soon the Aillwee Caves are signposted – a 900m cave system that includes an underground river and waterfall. Just before the road descends to Ballyvaughan, one of Ireland's most spectacular prehistoric monuments reveals itself. Standing 1.8m tall, the 5,000-year-old Poulnabrone portal dolmen is breathtaking. The surrounding karst landscape seems to elevate the tomb still higher and has the effect of making you feel (more) insignificant.

Now the road plunges through the spectacular Burren, past mournful Moneen Mountain to the right and Gleninag Mountain to the left. In between lies Galway Bay, which beckons like a siren. Bright and breezy Ballvaughan is a good place for a cuppa. Now the route turns sharp left onto the R477 – a poor surface but with magnificent perpetual views of the Atlantic. The road snakes along the foot of the mountains to Black Head where a lone lighthouse sends out its beacon. Continuing south, the Aran Islands once again appear. You may pass some climbers on the road hereabouts – Ailladie is one of Ireland's best rock-climbing sites. Soon, the road turns sharp left and climbs south-east to the N67 and a mighty 1km back to base.

12. Loop Head Peninsula Circuit, Clare

Kilkee – Newtown – Loop Head – Carrigaholt – Doonaha – Kilkee

Location:	County Clare
Grade:	2/3
Distance:	61km
Height gain:	475m
Duration:	3 to 3.5 hours
Verdict:	Stunning coastal route, with little traffic.

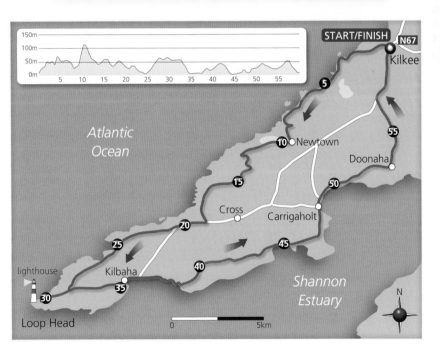

Start/finish

Kilkee, County Clare. Take the N68 south from Ennis or the N67 south from Lahinch.

Fishing trawlers in Carrigaholt, County Clare

I n this guide, there are views. And then there are views. Along this route is some of the finest coastal scenery to be found in the country and happily, there is very little traffic. The roads are good, with one short off-road section.

Route description

Starting beside the beach in the tourist town of Kilkee, take the coast road signposted from the western end of the beach. Almost immediately you are into the countryside and for about 12km this cycle is a breathtaking dash along the clifftops with the ever-present Atlantic heaving below. The ocean's deep blues, light greens and turquoises, capped by snow-white wavelets, make for a stupendous picture.

After about 4km, there is a sight that makes the famous Skelligs in County Kerry look like a prop for a film set. Bishop's Island has a 40m vertical cliff face on all sides with a few grassy acres on top. As helicopters did not exist in the ninth century, human endeavour saw the construction of a church, oratory and some clochauns (drystone-walled huts). It is truly incredible.

Leaving this wondrous sight, cycle along reasonable roads with just a few, or no, fields intervening to the sea. In early summer, gangs of choughs with their red boots congregate on the fence posts. The road meanders along the coast before diverging inland briefly on the way to Loop Head itself. A short diversion to the right leads to the Bridges of Ross, a spectacular sea arch (there were three before the sea consumed two).

At the halfway stage a really bad stretch of road is encountered. In fact, to call it a road is an exaggeration. Racers are a no-no here – get off and wheel – although hybrid bikes will be okay. This earthen and eroded tarmac section lasts for about 3km but ultimately gives way to a better road. Then the top of the Loop Head Lighthouse appears over the fields. There has been a lighthouse here since 1670 but the present structure dates from the 1850s. The views from the lighthouse are spectacular: south-west to the Dingle Peninsula and north to Achill Island. A great spot for a break.

Resuming, the road leads back to the village of Kilbaha. There is an option here to pick up the R487, which bisects the peninsula and leads back to Kilkee. Instead, take the coast road, L002, which leads to the pretty village of Carrigaholt where fishing boats bob up and down on the tide. The fifteenth-century Carrigaholt Castle stands like a sentinel at the entrance to the bay. After many cycles in March and April through slurry-impregnated air, the smell of salty air and seaweed is a delight to the nostrils.

As the road sweeps around one bend it nears the shore and the pebbles being pulled back by the retreating tide sound like a round of applause.

At Doonaha Cross the coastal section ends (though it can be lengthened by cycling to Querrin and then turning northwards towards Kilkee). Cycle north from the crossroads at Doonaha for 4km and intersect the R487. From here it is a straightforward run to the right (north) on a quality road back to base. A simply superb cycle!

13. Blennerville– Ballyheigue Return, Kerry

Blennerville – Tralee – Fenit – Ardfert – Ballyheigue – Lixnaw – Abbeydorney – Tralee – Blennerville

Location:	County Kerry
Grade:	3/4
Distance:	71km
Height gain:	392m
Duration:	3 to 4 hours.
Verdict:	Quiet roads and some lovely views of Dingle Peninsula.

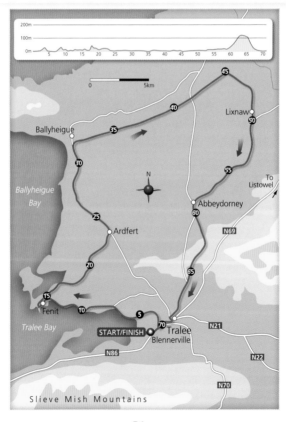

Start/finish

To reach Blennerville, drive south from Tralee on the N86.

Blennerville Windmill was built in 1800 to grind corn for local and export consumption. The village, south of Tralee, is well worth visiting for its eponymous windmill and hence is the start point of this route. It still functions as a commercial windmill, as well as having a visitor centre and restaurant. The route takes in stunning coastal views and history, from St Brendan the Navigator to the 1916 Easter Rising.

Blennerville Windmill, County Kerry

Route description

Cross the bridge at the windmill and immediately pick up a track which runs right into Tralee. The National Folk Theatre, Siamsa Tíre, is situated at the point where you make a left turn on the R874. Very soon that intersects the R551, which leads to the junction with the R558 after 1km.

Take this road, which ultimately leads to the village of Fenit. An island of the same name lies just offshore though it is connected to the land by a short sandspit. The island is reputed to be the birthplace of St Brendan the Navigator, who is commonly thought to have discovered America prior to Christopher Columbus.

There are great views along the Dingle Peninsula to Mount Brandon, which towers above, indifferent to the machinations of men.

Onwards on the coast road (a left turn if you're coming back from the island, otherwise straight on) gives fleeting vistas to the sea. This is partly because several fields separate the road from the coast along this stretch and partly because it is mainly due west and the route goes due north.

Next is the village of Ardfert, which is enticing for a coffee, though it is probably too early. By now on the R551, a brief diversion to take a look at Banna Strand offers itself up. One of the longest beaches in the country, it was the site of the failed attempt in 1916 by the nationalist Roger Casement to land a consignment of German rifles in the First World War in an effort to bolster the Easter Rising against British occupation.

Pushing northwards the busy R551 leads to the village of Ballyheigue. Just before that, however, turn right onto a small road running parallel to the R551 by now heading east. This is a very quiet road but, because it is built largely on a bog, it is a real strain for cycling. However, it affords you ample time to observe the multitudinous wild flowers along the way (presuming this is undertaken in the summer). The area is one of the most fertile in mountainous Kerry with incessant activity of tractors and slurry spreaders in the summer months. The Irish for a road or pathway across a bog is *togher* and, sure enough, just to the north lies the village of 'Tochár' – Causeway.

After 14km, the road comes to a junction. Turn right. Cross the recently built bridge over the Cashen River and press on to the village of Lixnaw. From here, head directly south on the R557, a routine stretch, to Abbeydorney.

On the far side of the village the road merges with the R556. There are several side roads that offer diversions from the traffic along here. So, after 1km, the main road veers to the right to Tralee, but intrepid cyclists may take the minor road straight ahead, which also leads to Tralee 8km distant. By this stage you are climbing. The ascent stops a few kilometres shy of the town and affords a tremendous descent and a great view along the peninsula and environs. Back in the sizeable town of Tralee, follow the signposts for Blennerville and the car.

14. Abbeyfeale to the Coast Loop

Abbeyfeale – Listowel – Ballybunion – Ballylongford –
Tarbert – Knockanure – Abbeyfeale

Location:	Counties Limerick and Kerry
Grade:	4
Distance:	92km
Height gain:	596m
Duration:	4 to 5 hours
Verdict:	Terrific route of varied woodland, coastal views and inland villages

Start/finish

Abbeyfeale in County Limerick.

Ballybunion beach, County Kerry

Not all the glories of Kerry are confined to the peninsulas and this route combines wooded roads, coastal cruising and, for the masochistically inclined, some tough ascents. Along a lovely wooded road there are several ups and downs but nothing of any significance. This route takes in Listowel, the home of one of Ireland's best-loved playwrights: John B. Keane. Most of the characters were based on country people who lived hereabouts. Keane's nuanced language captured the musical subtlety of the English spoken here.

Route description

Begin in the busy Limerick market town of Abbeyfeale just over the Kerry border. Take the R524 towards Glin but branch off to the left just after 1km onto the L1327. Pass through the village of Kilmorna and continue. The road will join the R523 coming from Athea. Continue on this road, which shortly joins the busy trunk road N69. Press on for 2km to reach the vibrant town of Listowel.

Too early for a coffee but many premises look enticing. Avoid the hectic R553 road to Ballybunion. Proceed along the N69 until a right turn onto William Street, followed after 100m by a left onto Market Street which leads onto Convent Street/Convent Road before branching off on the Greenville Road. The River Feale will be on the left across a few fields.

After 3.5km on a very quiet road take a sharp right towards the village of Oaghley.

Continue along here for just under 8km until intersecting the R554. In the distance to the right is Ballybunion Hill marked out by radio masts. Go left for 50m and then right on the R551 and Ballybunion lies 5km distant.

In summer, the population of the town swells with holidaymakers and day trippers taking advantage of the facilities, not least the wonderful beach in the maw of the Atlantic. This is a great spot for a break in any of several cafes and bars or just on the seafront. Suitably rested, take the coast road for the tiny village of Beal suitably updated with Wild Atlantic Way signage. There are great views over to the Loop Head Peninsula and the town of Kilrush. See if you can make out Scattery Island with its round tower and the remnants of six churches some dating from the sixth century.

In summer, the hedgerows are decorated with obelisks of purple loosestrife, fronds of meadowsweet and bells of foxgloves. By now at a decent height, the road sweeps along till the turning point for Carrig Island and one of the few out-and-back spurs in this guide. It is well worth it for the awesome sight of the fourteenth-century Carrigafoyle tower house nestling among the rushes of Carrig Island.

Retrace the 3km to the main road and go left to reach the village of Ballylongford, birthplace of the mercurial poet Brendan Kennelly: 'Broken castles tower, lost order's monument / Splendour crumbling in sun and rain.' Before long the town of Tarbert appears. This is the ferry stop for the trip across the estuary to Killimer in County Clare. Now take the very busy N69 towards Listowel but branch off after 3km toward Knockanure. This is an 11km ribbon of road that rises to a good height. At the T-junction, go left for 100m before a sharp right presents itself. Proceed for 2km until reaching another T-junction and go left. Retrace the cycle from earlier along the verdant Feale Valley to the start point at Abbeyfeale.

The Beal-to-Ballylongford road, County Kerry

15. Circuit of North Tipperary

*Thurles – Templemore – Roscrea – Moneygall –
Bouladuff – Thurles*

Location:	Counties Tipperary and Offaly
Grade:	3/4
Distance:	82km
Height gain:	530m
Duration:	4 to 4.5 hours
Verdict:	Some of the most gorgeous countryside of all the routes. Decent hills, but several poor roads.

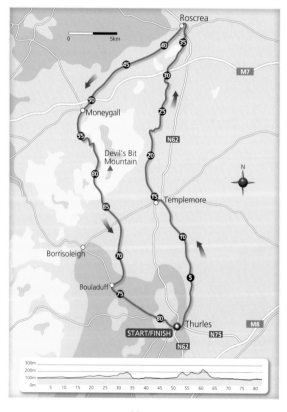

Start/finish

Thurles, County Tipperary. Park on the east side of town and look for the Bohernamona Road which intersects Mitchel Street/Loughtagalla Road on the left, past Kennedy's pub. The road here is one of the poorest in the entire book, but cycleable. And greatness awaits.

Cycling near the Devil's Bit Mountain, Roscrea, County Tipperary

This route extends far north into the midlands giving you an idea of the sheer scale of Munster. Roscrea to Castletownbere, for instance, is 270km. But that's for another time. The start point is the busy town of Thurles, home to the GAA's second biggest venue, Semple Stadium, where many a thriller has been played out over the years.

Route description

Leaving Thurles on the Bohernamona Road, the initial scenery along the way is interesting without being compelling. After 12km go right at a junction. Approaching Templemore, the road rises over a bridge under which the train tracks run to the nearby train station. As if on cue, a church bell peals: a rural setting straight out of a William Trevor story.

Continue on. The road leads to the fine town of Templemore with its wide streets and impressive buildings. The founder of the *Financial Times*, Brendan Bracken, was born here. Now at a T-junction, the road to the right leads directly to Roscrea on the N62. But where's the fun in taking the easy

The author outside Ollie Hayes' pub, Moneygall, County Offaly

way? Instead, veer left and proceed down the town for 500m and a right turn onto the L3216 heading towards Dunkerrin 17km distant. This road is much better than the first leg of this route.

Ignore a right turn at a fork after 5km. Stay straight for 3km more till a signpost to the right for Clonakeeny. A lovely, quiet road leads to a T-junction after 1km. Clonakeeny is to the left. Go north through the village and pass the Protestant St Burchin's Church on the left. At a T-Junction go left and after 500m go right. This narrow road climbs briefly before crossing, on a bridge, the M7 Dublin-to- Limerick motorway. Across the bridge, go right and head into the heritage town of Roscrea 5km distant. Many fine buildings attest to its heritage status and the town square would seem appropriate for a break or wait till Moneygall.

Back on board, leave south-westwards by Limerick Street which leads to Limerick Road and then the R445. This is serious stuff and the trucks thunder along. After 9km the village of Dunkerron is a welcome break. Continue along the road to Moneygall, which is in County Offaly, which, of course, is in Leinster. However, if the Tour de France can take in Belgium, Spain or Ireland, then this book can take in Leinster. Cycling, hillwalking and kayaking are not the arena for purists. Call it 'cycling licence'.

The forty-fourth president of the US, Barack Obama, visited his ancestral home of Moneygall in 2011 where he met his eighth cousin Henry Healy, now known as Henry the Eighth. They repaired to Ollie Hayes' pub for refreshments. No better place to stop in this village.

The next section is tricky. Take a sharp left at Obama cafe and continue along a gently rising poor road for 4km till you reach a crossroads. Take the left-hand turn which then curves right, like a scimitar, around to the foothills of Devil's Bit Mountain. The scenery here is magnificent, in as rustic a setting as you can get. The road slices though a forest and takes you due south. The L3228 and then the L3213 lead on to the tiny village of Drom. From here it is another 6km south to the crossroads of Bouladuff where the busier R498 is picked up and an 8km scoot back to base eastwards on a busy but good-quality road.

16. Gearagh Circuit, Cork

*Macroom – Kilmichael – Dunmanway – Ballineen – Enniskeane –
Newcestown – Kilmurry – Macroom*

Location:	County Cork
Grade:	3
Distance:	66km
Height gain:	306m
Duration:	3 to 3.5 hours
Verdict:	Quiet, rural cycling with many rivers to cross

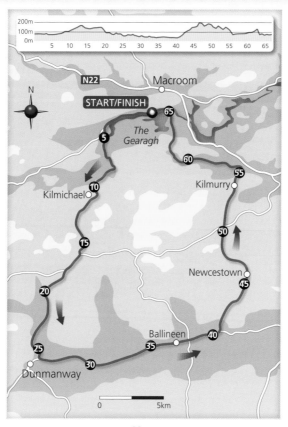

Start/finish

From Cork, drive towards Macroom on the N22. Just before the town, turn left onto the R584 and continue for about 4km to reach the entrance of the nature reserve of The Gearagh, where there is room for a couple of cars.

The Gearagh (from the Irish, *An Gaoire*, or 'wooded river') is home to numerous rare species of plant and animal life. It is well worth a tour before or after this cycle. This route also takes in historic Kilmichael, scene of perhaps the most famous encounter of the War of Independence in 1920 when an IRA flying column under Tom Barry ambushed a British army patrol and killed seventeen soldiers. A week later Cork city centre was burnt down by the Black and Tans in reprisal.

Route description

Turn left/west onto the R584 for about 3km, then branch left to take the southbound R587. After 2km the road crosses a bridge over the River Lee, a mere stream here really, compared to the better-known powerful downstream force. Very soon, the road passes through Kilmichael. Continue on to the village of Shanlaragh before fetching up in the busy market town of Dunmanway. A good spot for a coffee, if required.

Cycling towards The Gearagh, County Cork

Back on the saddle, it is a long stretch of 12km on the R586 to the villages of Ballineen and Enniskean – effectively one long conurbation. The usual compensation in these scenarios applies, though: a very good surface which allows for a speed of upwards of 35km/h.

After another 2km take the L2009, which appears on the left. Now the roads are quiet again and with a good surface. Many ups and downs on rolling farmland provides some thrilling cycling here. After 5km the village of Newcestown materialises. Pick up the L2008 by taking the second left after the church. The next node is Kilmurry which, after the initial 2km north-west of Newcestown, is 8km directly north. The L2008 becomes the L2004 when it crosses the busy R585 east–west road.

A dive or two downhill and an upwards pull to the village of Kilmurry and it is time for a quick break. Then head downhill towards the N22 Cork-to-Killarney road, but avoid at all costs. Instead, veer left towards Warrenscourt Wood and after 1km veer right across a small bridge. This is a lovely wooded section that runs straight for 4km. Avoid three left-hand turns, and heading north, climb briefly before descending on the Sleaveen Road, which crosses The Gearagh and intersects the busy R584. From here the car is 1km to the left/west.

17. Doneraile Figure of Eight, Cork & Limerick

Doneraile – Ardpatrick – Skenakilla Cross Roads – Castletownroche – Skenakilla Cross Roads – Doneraile

Location:	Counties Cork and Limerick
Grade:	3
Distance:	64km
Height gain:	690m
Duration:	3 to 3.5 hours
Verdict:	An excellent route of quiet rural cycling

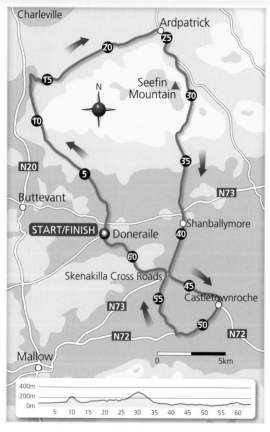

Start/finish

Begin in the village of Doneraile, 7km east of the N20 Cork-to-Limerick road between Buttevant and Mallow.

This figure-of-eight route takes in some beautiful countryside: forests, railway crossings, quiet back roads and sleepy villages. This is the polar opposite of cycling in busy city traffic: cool mountain air rushes into the lungs making for a turbo-charged cycle. Doneraile itself is home to the park of the same name. The 400-acre estate had its origins in the seventeenth century with the construction of the stately house, and contains some larch trees that are 300 years old.

Route description

Park in Doneraile's main street and cycle northwards on the R581 until Brough crossroads about 2km away. Go straight through for the L1328, and cycle along for 3km on not-so-great roads. At the fork take the right-hand option. The road climbs for 3km or so through hedged-in fields and farms before emerging at a junction. To the left is Ballyhea. However, cycle straight on to the railway crossing (there is also a railway crossing leading to Ballyhea, but that's not the route). This is a junction on the Cork-to-Dublin railway and at least fourteen trains per day pass through, so be prepared to wait for the signalman to raise the gates before you can proceed. Once across, the road turns briefly south before resuming eastwards along the northern flank of the Ballyhoura Mountains. Another book could be written about the world-class mountain bike trails of the Ballyhouras. It has trails of 6km, 17km, 35km, 42km and 51km.

Shortly, you arrive on the R512. Straight ahead lies the well-known town of Kilmallock. However, this route goes right, to the charming village of Ardpatrick – a good spot for a break. Two kilometres after Ardpatrick take the right-hand option in the fork. By now on the eastern side of the Ballyhoura Mountains and the Glenanaar Forest, the road climbs steeply for a few kilometres to a picnic area from where there is simply a superb view of the valley below. Nestled in the folds of the hills is the mock-Victorian Castle Oliver which stands on 20,000 acres and reputedly has the country's largest wine cellar with 55,000 bottles.

Fighting off a thirst, press on for a wonderful 6km downhill charge through the edge of the forest and onto the N73. This very busy road (great surface, of course) takes you to Skenakilla Cross Roads 4km south. Here, take the sharp left to the lovely, hilly village of Castletownroche.

Now cycle 4km south-west on the N72 before taking a sharp right (signposted for Doneraile) which will lead you once more to Skenakilla Cross Roads. It is a bit confusing here: the road you need is 100m north on the N73. This left turn leads directly back to Doneraile along tree-lined roads.

18.Cork–Robert'sCove Return

Frankfield – Ballygarvan – Riverstick – Belgooly – Minane Bridge – Robert's Cove – Carrigaline – Douglas – Frankfield

Location:	County Cork
Grade:	3
Distance:	58km
Height gain:	784m
Duration:	3 to 3.5 hours
Verdict:	Some of the most gorgeous countryside of all, with decent hills, but several poor roads

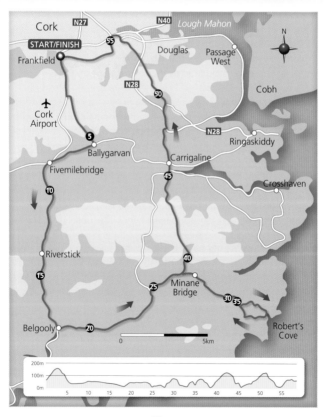

Start/finish

Start at the Bull McCabe's bar on the airport road from Cork city. There is ample parking at the back of the pub.

With not many beaches on the doorstep of Cork city, the intrepid cyclist must search out a decent route while still leaving enough in the tank for the swim itself. So to the destination of Robert's Cove. The route is hilly and on busy roads but gets you to the sea.

Route description

Leaving the car park, continue up the hill towards the airport. There is a cycle track but it is in poor condition. After 1km the traffic eases dramatically as most of it turns right into the airport. Go left at the roundabout. The road bends to the right after 100m. Continue straight ahead (the Rathmacullig West road). This is of reasonable quality and descends rapidly to a T-junction on the R603.

Go right, through the tiny village of Ballygarvan, which comes up after 200m, and continue to the junction of Fivemilebridge. This route continues to the left towards Kinsale on the R600. The road has been widened and landscaped, which is a pity in a way as the previous road meandered through an old wood. Progress, it is called. The road crosses the Owenabue River for the first of two times in this cycle. It flows east to Carrigaline and enters the sea at Drake's Pool.

Riverstick is next up after 11km, followed by Belgooly, dominated by an old flour mill. Turn left here between the Huntsman's and Coleman's bars on the R611 signposted for Carrigaline/Minane Bridge. After 6.5km between green fields and leafy ditches there is a signpost for Minane Bridge. Turning right at a private house, which looks like it is in the middle of the road, continue for 2.5km on the L3210 to Minane Bridge and go straight through. The road climbs briefly before descending to Robert's Cove which is signposted. If the weather is fine, take a well-deserved dip on a lovely beach.

Back on the way, take the road heading south along the cove. This swings inland and rejoins the road that entered Robert's Cove by taking the first right. Now, retrace the route to Minane Bridge and turn right shortly after the village towards Carrigaline. There is a 100m climb for 4km on this stretch before the road dives into Carrigaline.

Continue straight across three roundabouts to join the N28 for Cork, just for 1km and then take the L6477 on the right. This rises for 1km before a sweeping descent goes to the heart of Douglas via Maryborough Hill. Go right at the roundabout, and cycle to the next traffic lights. Go left here and after 1km turn right for Grange. Pass through this suburb and the next, Frankfield, before forking to the left through Frankfield Business Park (the R851). The start/finish point is 1km further along.

19. Kilmallock–Doon Circuit, Limerick

Kilmallock – Hospital – Pallasgreen – Doon – Cappamore – Caherconlish – Ballyneety – Bruff – Kilmallock

Location:	County Limerick
Grade:	3/4
Distance:	86km
Height gain:	570m
Duration:	4 to 5 hours
Verdict:	Very flat countryside. Very good for going through the gears on long flat stretches.

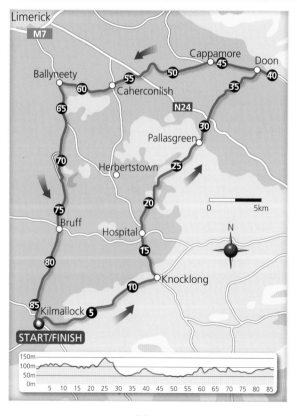

Start/finish

Kilmallock, County Limerick: from Limerick city, the most direct route to take is the R512.

The flat nature of this cycle is reminiscent of Holland. In Ireland, you get used to fabulous descents and eye-bulging ascents. The highest climb on this route is no more than 50m. Very long, straight roads indicate the dearth of major features in the landscape. There are no mountains sweeping down to the sea, no mighty rivers thundering past. The Ballyhoura Mountains and, farther east, the Galtees are still there, of course, but distant, just a reminder that you are in a mountainous country. And you'll need that reminder. What there is in abundance is rolling green fields and hedgerows teeming with birdlife. And village after village.

At St John's Castle, Kilmallock, County Limerick

Route description

South-west out of the busy market town of Kilmallock, pick up the R515 road for Knocklong. A pleasant 13km of relatively anonymous character (except for the curiously named village of Elton) whooshes by. A sharp left turn now on the R513 and you aim for the next node: Hospital.

The roads around here are fairly quiet. Continue to the end of the village on the long street before ascending to the right on the L8502. This is the toughest (and virtually the only) climb on the circuit, lasting about 1.5km. Next comes the village of Kilteely, followed soon after on the same road by Old Pallasgreen and then swiftly, Pallasgreen.

From here take the L1152 roughly north. It crosses the Limerick-to-Tipperary road and becomes the L1135, which goes to the attractive village of Doon. Just before Doon, cross Dead River. Several fine-looking pubs entice the thirsty or scone-seeking cyclist. Perhaps a bit early for that as we have completed just over 30km out of 88km.

Retrace the route for several kilometres here, west on the R505, to get back on track for Cappamore – again, long streets are the hallmark of this village, indicative of the flat hinterland.

At the end of the village push on for the next node of Caherconlish. Before this village it is necessary to recross the very busy Limerick-to-Tipperary road. Directly across the road is the route, which forks after 50m. Take the right turn on the unnamed, unnumbered road which leads right into Caherconlish on what is the prettiest section of the entire cycle. Heavily wooded side roads, virtually traffic-free, meander though a rustic setting. Would that it could last! Instantly in Caherconlish the Norman character of the town strikes you. There are de Barra and de Courcy names over business premises and a mock round tower. This is a fine spot to stop for a coffee before the final and busiest section.

Ballyneety is the next port of call, 6km west, again on an unnumbered road, but signposted – always a help. A sharp turn left (south) follows on to the busy R512 and an 11km run to the very attractive village of Bruff on good quality roads. Three kilometres before Bruff is one of Ireland's most famous prehistoric sites: Lough Gur. Finally, continue south on the R512 for 10km to the start/finish point of Kilmallock.

20. Copper Coast Loop, Waterford

Dungarvan – Stradbally – Bunmahon – Annestown – Fennor –
Tramore – Fennor – Dunhill – Bunmahon – Dungarvan

Location:	County Waterford
Grade:	3/4
Distance:	73km
Height gain:	893m
Duration:	3 to 4 hours
Verdict:	Beautiful coastal route on way out, with many hills on the return leg

Start/finish

From Cork, take the N25 to Dungarvan. Drive into the town and pick up the R675 on the east side of Dungarvan and drive for 5km due east. Just before the road turns sharply northwards, with Clonea Bay behind you at this point, there is a minor road to the right leading down to a beach. It is signposted for Comeraghs View B&B. There is parking along here for a few cars.

One of Ireland's unsung treasures, the Copper Coast evokes long-ago memories of the mining industry without, perhaps, the allure of the Mosquito Coast or the Gold Coast. Copper mining has long since ceased as it has far down the coast at Allihies on the Beara Peninsula.

Route description

At the start, the road is in poor condition for a few kilometres. In fact, it isn't at all apparent where the road can possibly go as it is hemmed in by the sea on one side and a high ridge on the other. Anyway, the road is there! Cross the wide bridge under which flows the River Dalligan and continue upwards to the left on a gentle incline for a while.

Very soon the village of Stradbally materialises (one of many in the country). The views of the Atlantic for which this route is renowned reveal themselves. A bracing, salty wind will probably greet you here as you progress to the next point on the route, the village of Bunmahon. The high roads into the town are of good quality and it is possible to really

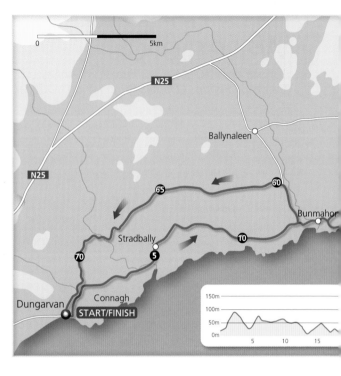

Thatched cottage at Dunhill, County Waterford

move through the gears if desired. Bunmahon's long sandy beach is a magnet for surfers and the town itself is a hub of water-based activities in the summer.

Press on to Annestown, 8km distant. The roads could be better here, but the traffic is light, which compensates. Seagulls glide past as you whizz along through rolling farmland and past holiday houses. The road now cuts inland for a while before turning east at the village of Fennor. The halfway point of Tramore looms up ahead. Was that really 33km? The town is a sprawling metropolis compared to the quiet villages just passed through.

There are a number of cafes in the town to grab a quick cuppa before it's back on the bike. In truth, the outward journey is the better half of this

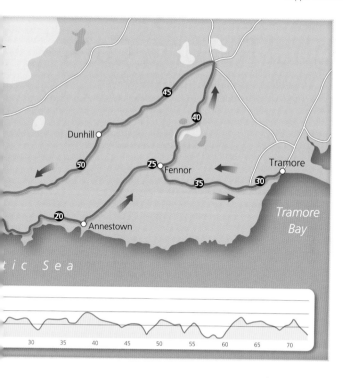

On the road near Annestown, County Waterford

route as the return is away from the Atlantic.

Return the 4km on the R675 to Fennor and turn right in the village. Stay left at two junctions and pass a small lake on the left. After another 1km there is a large junction. Go left. After 3km the quaint village of Dunhill with its thatched cottage appears over a hill. Continue southwest with many rises and falls till the sound of the waves at Bunmahon.

From Bunmahon pick up the R675 again and head north for 3km before the road veers sharply left and carries the rider all the way home.

21. Castlemartyr–Youghal Return, Cork

Castlemartyr – Mogeely – Killeagh – Mount Uniacke –
Youghal – Ballymacoda – Knockadoon – Garryvoe – Castlemartyr

Location:	County Cork
Grade:	3
Distance:	62km
Height gain:	530m
Duration:	2.5 to 3 hours
Verdict:	Beautiful inland and coastal route with attractive villages along the way.

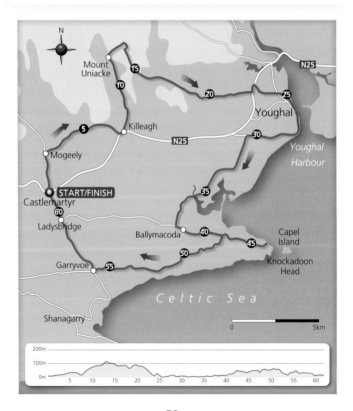

Start/finish

Begin in the village of Castlemartyr, 32km east of Cork. You will find parking space on the main street.

If rolling hills seem to be a prevailing theme in this guide, it's because there are a lot of them in Munster. And this route seems to have more than most. Many areas have a concentration of villages and hamlets to discover. Scarcely have you passed through one before another appears – very true of this route. The villages of east Cork, while not as busy as their illustrious west Cork cousins, nevertheless have inherent attractions themselves, including the East Cork Early Music Festival in Killeagh and Midleton every September, for example.

Arriving at Mount Uniacke from Killeagh en route to Youghal, County Cork

Route description

Instead of taking the road to Youghal take a sharp left heading towards Mogeely on an unnumbered road. Reach Mogeely after a humongous 2km. Time for a coffee break! At Mogeely, cross the disused railway line which used to connect Cork to Youghal.

Take a sharp right here towards Killeagh which lies 5km distant. So far so good. You cycle through gorgeous countryside in this section. With

77

7km knocked off, take a sharp turn northwards (left) on the L3806 towards the curiously named hamlet of Mount Uniacke. The road on the left is the eastern margin of one of the most beautiful woods in the country: Glenbower Wood.

At Mount Uniacke take a right turn for 1km before turning right again and heading south-eastwards towards Youghal. This resort town is known for its long sandy beaches and was once the destination for thousands of Corkonian families on weekend excursions. The town is the point at which the River Blackwater enters the sea. Take a coffee here on the breezy promenade.

Thirst sated, join the R634 for 3km on the south of the town. The road bends to the left and soon take a sharp left onto the R633. There is a fine viewing platform here for the nature reserve of Ballyvergan Marsh. The village of Ballymacoda lies 8km along this not-great road but the bad surface is compensated for by minimal traffic.

Continue for an extra 4km to the sea at Knockadoon. From here there is a great view of the nature reserve of Capel Island, which is home to a significant colony of cormorants. Retracing the route to Ballymacoda, turn left after 1.5km on a road that leaves a lot to be desired. Watch out for signposts for the caravan hub of Garryvoe 4km farther on. From Garryvoe, turn right on the R632 and head back to base directly north via Ladysbridge.

22. South-East Tipperary Circuit

Clonmel – Fethard – Mullinahone – Ninemilehouse –
Carrick-on-Suir – Clonmel

Location:	County Tipperary
Grade:	3
Distance:	76km
Height gain:	640m
Duration:	4 to 4.5 hours
Verdict:	Some fine hills to give a great workout; very wooded towards end.

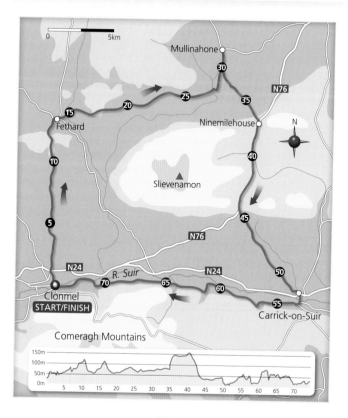

Start/finish

Start at the busy market town of Clonmel, County Tipperary. Mary Street car park on the riverbank has free parking.

On the approach to Fethard, County Tipperary

The prevailing theme for this route is one of Ireland's most famous mountains: Slievenamon (*Sliabh na mBan*, or 'mountain of the women'). It is reputedly named after the women who competed in a race to win the hand of Irish legendary hero Finn mac Cumhail in the mists of time. Ride west of it, north of it, east of it and south of it. This is a route with multiple options. Enticing roads lead off at several points. This route is just a taster of what's on offer. You may want to come back again and again to try different options.

Route description

From the centre of Clonmel, head northwards on the busy R689 to the medieval walled town of Fethard 14km distant. A beautiful spot for a coffee, but far too early. Cycle to the town square before veering off to the right and the R692. Quiet roads of limited elevation soon lead to the village of Mullinahone. Retrace the route for a few kilometres until you pick up the R690 heading south.

After 6km, turn right at the T-junction onto the extremely busy N76 Clonmel-to-Kilkenny Road. After 7km of superb road surface and exhausting exhaust, turn left onto the R696 to the major town of Carrick-on-Suir – home of one of Ireland's most famous cyclists, Sean Kelly. Kelly cut his teeth on the roads around the Comeragh Mountains and when you see them, you will realise why they were a great foundation to his talent. The meandering Suir cuts through the town like a velvet blade and rushes beneath the town's splendid bridges. Definitely stop for a coffee here.

Entering the town, take the second exit on the roundabout and follow this road, called the New Road, for 500m and a right turn onto New Street. A quick dog-leg (right, left) leads onto the bridge. Across the bridge turn right on the R680. The valley stretching out below of rolling pastureland is surely one of Ireland's most beautiful. Norman castles dot the countryside, often with commanding views of the hinterland. By now in the distance, Slievenamon watches over, like a mother.

This section is predominantly native woodland: oak, ash, beech and alder jostle with each other beside the road.

Continue west and pass the infamously difficult Tikincor Hill on the left, which is worth a diversion for those with vast lungs. Otherwise, press on home to Clonmel. Do not cross the beautiful arched Sir Thomas's Bridge 3km outside the town. Instead, approaching the bridge, stay left on the R680 which brings you right into town. This road leads to a roundabout. Across the bridge to the right is the Mary Street car park.

23. Glen of Aherlow Loop, Tipperary

Galbally – Tipperary – Glen of Aherlow – Lisvarrinane – Anglesborough – Galbally

Location:	Counties Limerick and Tipperary
Grade:	2
Distance:	47km
Height gain:	507m
Duration:	2 to 2.5 hours
Verdict:	A magnificent cycle for a Sunday morning.

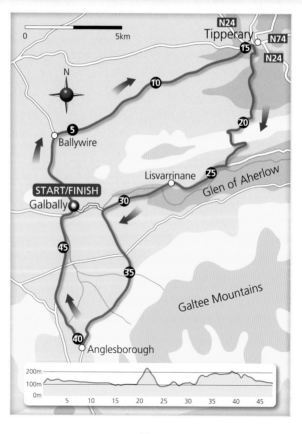

Start/finish

The start point is the handsome village of Galbally, County Limerick, with its spacious square.

This route just about qualifies for the mid-range but it makes up in the spectacular what it lacks in the distance. Galbally is one of several start points for the Glen of Aherlow walks. Another is the nearby Moor Abbey – a beautiful ruined Franciscan friary on the banks of the Aherlow River, which flows down from the Galtee Mountains. The Galtee range extends west to east for around 30km. It is hugely popular with hillwalkers who relish the steep climbs, glaciated cirques and wonderful woods on the lower fringes.

In the Glen of Aherlow, County Tipperary

Route description

Head north-west from Galbally on the R662 and turn east after 4km. By now into County Tipperary, it is a relatively straightforward run to Tipperary town, which lies 12km distant. At the start of the town, take the road to the right (the R664), Bridge Street and then Station Road and pass through the level crossing. The road turns right, then left, before climbing for 3km to a T-junction. Left, on another terrific road to Bansha, is for another day. For now, swing right in the direction of Lisvarrinane and climb through Bansha Woods. This leads into the Glen of Aherlow proper – closer to the Galtees. Here, Slievenamuck Mountain forms the northernmost side of the Glen of Aherlow. Just before the viewing area is Aherlow House Hotel, which merits a quick coffee for the tremendous views of the glen. Opposite the hotel, across the glen, is the imposing mountain of Galtymore, which is one of the biggest in Ireland at 919m, and the County High Point for both Tipperary and Limerick.

Sweep downwards to a T-junction at the hamlet of Newtown. Go right towards Lisvarrinane on the R663. The sense of peace that attends the Glen of Aherlow is pleasing to the soul. On a spring day with the daffodils nodding in the ditches, the cows ruminating in the fields and the hedgerows alive with birdlife, it attains a kind of rustic bliss. Scant traffic bothers the cyclist.

There are several campsites and caravan sites along the way indicating the popularity of the valley. This is one of the most attractive wooded cycles in the country on roads that are, by and large, of good quality. Next up is the village of Lisvarrinane, which itself is a start point for several walking routes in the valley. A short way along is Moor Abbey. Go left before the bridge (straight ahead lies Galbally). By now heading south, this road curves around for 8km to the pretty village of Anglesborough – the highest village in the range. From here upwards, only the hardiest eke out a living on the slopes of the mountains. This is yet another start point for Aherlow walks. In the village take a 90-degree turn to the right and cycle northwards. After 2km, meet the R662 – bear right – and after 5km, reach Galbally and the conclusion of this wonderful cycle. Too short. Go around again.

24. Kildorrery–Galbally Figure of Eight

Kildorrery – Ballylanders – Galbally – Kilfinane – Kildorrery

Location:	Counties Cork and Limerick
Grade:	3
Distance:	71km
Height gain:	673m
Duration:	3 to 3.5 hours
Verdict:	A fine country cycle on the border of Cork and Limerick.

Start/finish

Kildorrery, 12km west of Mitchelstown in County Cork. You will find car parking space on the main street.

The landscape on this route is predominantly open pastureland but because of the numerous hills involved there are some very attractive views. An interesting diversion along the way is Griston Bog, a nature reserve and bird sanctuary run by the Ballyhoura Heritage and Environment group. Wooden walkways traverse a marsh and bogland and offer great views of the birdlife including sandpiper, curlews, dippers and herons – depending on the time of year.

Route description

From Kildorrery's main street, head east towards Mitchelstown on the N73 before branching off after 4.5km on the R512 in the direction of Kilmallock. This is a lovely quiet road on a good surface. There are a number of thatched cottages in the area affirming its charm. The massive flank of the Galtee Mountain Range is visible to the right about 10km away.

After 5km a junction presents itself. Kilfinnane is to the left but our route lies straight ahead towards Ballylanders. After 5km, you may choose to stop off and visit Griston Bog. Carry on for a further 5km to reach Ballylanders.

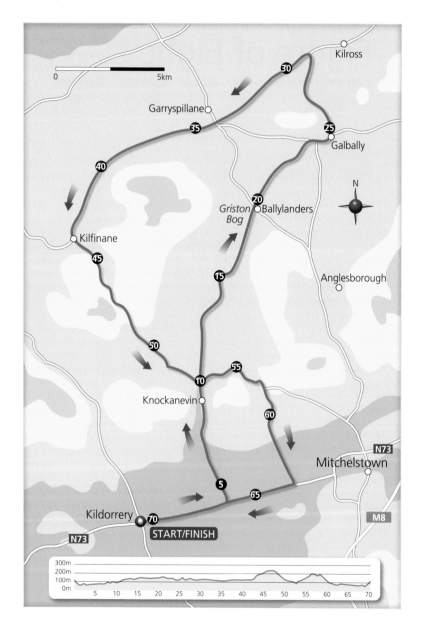

Go left for a few hundred metres before a sharp right, which, after 5km, will take you to the pleasant village of Galbally. This is a good spot for a break – there are a couple of fine pubs here and an Indian takeaway.

Leave on the northern route out of the village, the R662 towards Tipperary. After 4km take a sharp left, the L1511, and a really long, straight road to Kilfinane, 14km away. This stretch is a bit monotonous, but never fear, much better awaits.

The village of Kilfinane finally comes to the rescue. This village is the home of the Ballyhoura Development Ltd. Judging by the state of the village – flower boxes, brightly painted buildings, public shrubberies and seating, well-placed information boards – anything this group turns its hand to is likely to be well done. A great spot for a break if it suits, at this point.

Back on board the bike, take the R517 to the south-west of the village. This is known as Wood Road and it lives up to its name in spectacular fashion. A good-quality surface enables the rider to build up a decent speed under the branches of the oaks and beeches whose branches hang down over the road as if enticing you into the woods. There are a couple of fairly steep climbs in the next 9km section to a junction you passed through earlier. This is the confluence of the rivers Sheep and Keale. Stay on the R517 towards Mitchelstown. However, after 3km swing right, heading south through open fields and past a few electricity pylons. This is a lovely quiet road that has a fine descent on a good surface. It brings you back on to the main Mitchelstown-to-Kildorrery Road, the N73, and a right-hand turn will lead directly back to the car, which lies 8km away.

25. Kinsale–Kilmurry Return, Cork

Kinsale–Ballinadee–Innishannon–Kilmurry–Crookstown–Upton – Innishannon – Kinsale

Location:	County Cork
Grade:	3/4
Distance:	77km
Height gain:	1,055m
Duration:	4 to 4.5 hours
Verdict:	Stunning route in places, poor road surface for 5km, but great ascents and descents.

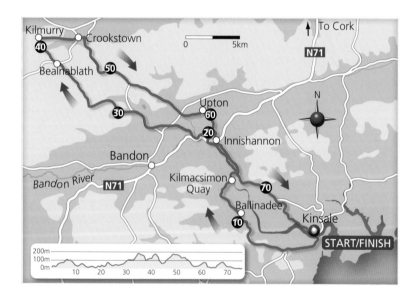

Start/finish

The start point is the bridge just south of Kinsale on the road to Garrets-town. There is ample room before the bridge for several cars.

Crossing Duggan Bridge, Kinsale, County Cork

There are tremendous views of the Bandon River along much of this route and some lovely villages in which to grab a coffee. Innishannon, though very busy, is beautifully situated on the river. Returning on the third leg of the route affords a carefree downhill spree.

Route description

Cross the bridge and pass the ruined tower house on the right. This is the R600. Along the road after 6km pass the turn-off on the left for the Old Head of Kinsale. After another few hundred metres there is a right turn off the main road. This is the L3223. A good-surfaced, meandering, hilly road follows to reach the village of Ballinadee. At the first fork in the village take the right-hand option. This leads past Kilmacsimon Quay and touches base again with the River Bandon – a companion for half of the entire route. From here to Innishannon the road surface is awful, though the views of the river through the banks of reeds or the trees are splendid. The village of Innishannon is charming, in spite of the traffic.

Cross the bridge into the village and take the first left, a climb that brings you past fields of daffodils (January to March), which is an interesting variation on the standard crops grown in Ireland. The next main stop is Kilmurry, some 21km distant. There are many side roads that look similar to the desired option. It is more or less in a straight line from Innishannon. The first point of confusion occurs after 6km – go right. The next confusing point is after another 2.5km – go left. After another 4.5km, take a sharp right. The road now runs straight to Bealnablath, 5km distant. The surface is reasonable for the most part. Cyclists unfamiliar with Irish history may be surprised at the massive memorial at Bealnablath. It is to the memory of Michael Collins of the Free State army who was killed in August 1922 by a sniper for the anti-Treaty republicans during the Civil War.

The village of Kilmurry is 3km farther along the road, which has a couple of challenging climbs. This is a good spot for a break as it is the turning point of the route.

Batteries recharged, take the right-hand turn towards the next node: Crookstown. As this is high ground there are some stunning views of the green fields left and right as you plummet onwards. Pass through Crookstown and take the second right towards Bandon, the R590. After 6km the road divides. Take the left-hand option, the L2235. As there is still a decent bit of height and the road is good there is scope for some fast downhill cycling. Next is the village of Upton. Continue through a T-junction and swing around to the right, before another stunning 4km section downhill into Innishannon.

The last leg again travels above the River Bandon to Kinsale. Turn left on arriving in Innishannon and mount the hill facing you after 200m. There follows a magnificent cycle for several kilometres on the R605 through a wood above the river. At the first obvious fork take the right-hand option, which leads back to the car.

26. Cork City–Cobh Return

Cork – Passage West – Glenbrook – Cobh – Glenbrook – Passage West – Cork

Location:	County Cork
Grade:	2
Distance:	50km
Height gain:	458m
Duration:	2.5 to 3 hours
Verdict:	Diverse route incorporating city, river, country roads and coast.

Start/finish

Albert Quay, Cork city centre, where the north and south branches of the River Lee merge. There are several public car parks nearby.

This is one of only two cycles in this guide to incorporate a ferry trip so, for novelty value alone, it is worth it. Throw in some riverside cycling and a wildlife park and it is very much worth it. The route takes us to Cobh, formerly Queenstown, a town steeped in history, having been the departure point for emigrants from the Great Famine of 1841–45. It was also the last port of call for RMS *Titanic* which sank in 1912 in the north Atlantic with the loss of over 1,500 lives. Cobh is a pretty town and, if you have time, try and visit the former prison at Spike Island, Ireland's Alcatraz – minus the sharks.

Route description

Cycle south to Victoria Road and take the second left, Centre Park Road. At the end of this leafy road you reach the River Lee. Turn right and cycle along the avenue till you come to a pier at Blackrock village. Continue on the road above the pier till you reach Blackrock castle.

On the riverside, a track leads along the shore of Lough Mahon (Cork's inner harbour) before intersecting with another track. Go left here, then take the R610 at Rochestown. Go left on the main road opposite the Rochestown Inn, for 2km till, at Hop Island, a track appears on the left.

Old railway bridge at Rochestown in Cork

This is the route of the old Passage West railway to the city. It is a beautiful walk or cycle to the village of Passage West. Just after the village at Glenbrook is the roll-on roll-off ferry. Used mainly by commuters from the Cobh area who work across the river, it saves a round trip of about 60km. The ferry takes bikes for a return price of €2. The crossing is rapid and interesting for the skill of the navigating pilot in landing the craft at a small pier on the opposite side.

Once across, turn right towards Cobh. On the approach to the town giant ships' derricks stand in deserted shipyards and if you half-close your eyes and have an accommodating imagination you can easily picture them as the alien beings from H. G. Wells' *War of the Worlds* about to wreak havoc on the earthlings. Time for a coffee here in any number of pubs or cafes.

Continue through the town to the east and a very steep climb exiting the town. The road quality is dire from here on till you return to the ferry

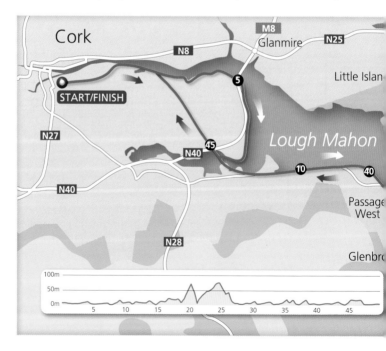

On the track from Blackrock Castle, Cork

but the roads are very quiet! Cycle past Cuskinny Marsh and on to Marlogue Wood where a left turn brings you to the north of Great Island. From here it is a straight run back to the fifteenth-century tower house of Belvelly Castle. Just over the bridge to the right is the world-famous Fota Wildlife Park, which has many exotic species including giraffes, a hippopotamus, tigers and several species of monkey.

Instead of crossing the bridge, take the road to the left which, after a few kilometres, brings you once again to the ferry. Retrace the route as far as the trackway opposite the Rochestown Inn. However, this time continue on straight instead of turning right. Cross the South Ring Road on a bridge and continue on the track which brings you back to Páirc Uí Chaoimh beside the river. Take the next left, Centre Park Road, to return to the start point.

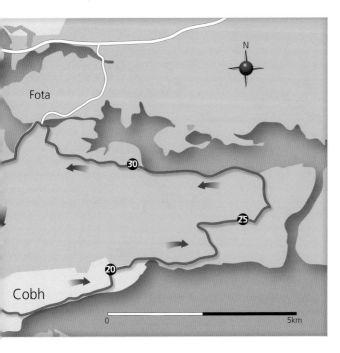

27. Ballyvourney–Kealkill Loop, Cork & Kerry

Ballyvourney – Kilgarvan – Kealkill – Ballingeary – Ballyvourney

Location:	Counties Cork and Kerry
Grade:	4/5
Distance:	86km
Height gain:	1,374m
Duration:	4.5 to 5.5 hours
Verdict:	Outstanding route through the mountains on the Cork/Kerry border. Poor roads.

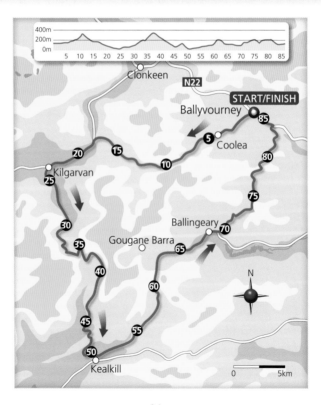

Start/finish

Start at the village of Ballyvourney on the N22 Cork-to-Killarney road. There are several roads off to the left: take the one beside a bridge at the Killarney end.

Quietness is the watchword here, with just a handful of cars encountered on the whole trip. Magnificence is another: this is a remote, wooded route, but unfortunately has some poor roads.

Route description

Cross the bridge at the Killarney end of Ballyvourney and immediately turn right. The road soon carries you to the village of Coolea. You are now in the heart of the Gaeltacht and more likely to hear a '*Dia dhuit*' than a 'good morning'.

Continue through Coolea. Ignore a turn to the right. Some tough climbs ensue, with giant wind turbines for company, slicing through the air like giant scythes. At the next obvious fork, go right. The superb road pays out before you on a largely deserted landscape: purple heather, woodland and bogland with countless streams and rivers. The road is not at a great height but it feels like it. You think this beauty can't go on, but on it goes.

Cycling above Coolea, County Kerry

Very soon you arrive at the Top of the Coom bar which claims to be Ireland's highest pub. (The claim is disputed with Johnnie Fox's in Dublin.) The road now plunges through wild countryside, turning and twisting in the Roughty Valley. By now into Kerry, this section of the road terminates at Morley's Bridge and intersects the busier R569. The River Roughty thunders under the bridge and there is a famous salmon pool here.

Turn left. Soon you arrive in the village of Kilgarvan. Towards the end of the village there is a left turn for Bantry. Take it. This is the spectacular Borlin Valley. The road is very quiet, and, though it is poorly surfaced, you won't care. Halfway along is a rocky outcrop where you can take in glorious views of the valley by standing out on a perch. The road winds onwards and upwards and though you are quite high, the climbing is easy.

Take a break at the col and gasp at the amazing valley that lies before you. Pockets of green fields reclaimed from the bog stand out like green windows. Descend and after 8km take a very sharp left at the Knockaneacosduff marker. Now climb and descend for a while, to reach the village of Kealkill. Take the R584 from here, which leads to Keimaneigh Pass and farther on to Ballingeary. Off to the left is the National Park of Gougane Barra, which is well worth a visit on another day. One kilometre after Ballingeary turn left and begin a tough ascent towards base. After 3km take a 90-degree right turn and almost immediately a left. There is a T-junction after 2km. Go left for 3.5km to another T-junction. Turn right to reach Ballymakeery. Turn left and follow the road for about 2km to return to Ballyvourney and your car.

28. Cork/Kerry Circuit: Coomholla–Kilgarvan

Coomholla – Priest's Leap – Kilgarvan – Borlin Valley – Coomholla

Location:	Counties Cork and Kerry
Grade:	4/5
Distance:	56km
Height gain:	1,202m
Duration:	2.5 to 3.5 hours
Verdict:	Difficult mountain route, with challenging climbs and great descents: superb

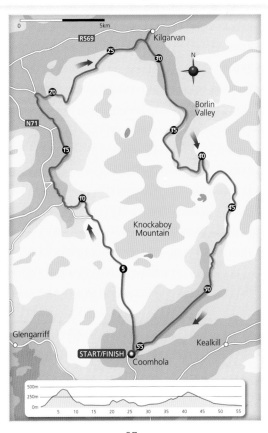

Start/finish

Leave the N71 Bantry-to-Glengarriff Road at the signpost for Coomholla Bridge. The bridge is 2km inland in a heavily wooded area far from the madding crowd. Park in the vicinity of the bridge.

This road has exceptionally difficult climbing at the outset, which is not easy if you're fresh out of the car. It is advisable to warm up with a 10km cycle before you attempt this. However, it also includes what is probably the finest stretch of cycling road in the country.

Route description

From Coomholla Bridge, the desired road is a little to the left and then right. From here it is 6km to the top of Priest's Leap on the Cork/Kerry border; though shorter than, say, the Conor Pass on the Dingle Peninsula, this is a much harder route.

A gruelling climb with various gradients ensues. There are occasional flat sections before ever-tougher road 'cliffs' ahead of you. Suffice it to say, you won't be admiring the countryside. The start point is 28m above sea level and the col is at 445m or, to put it another way, 417m ascent in just under 6km. This is the first of two category 2 climbs on the route and it has an overall gradient of 7 per cent.

Many gasps later, you arrive at the col known as Priest's Leap, a good spot for a very well-earned rest. The name derives from a mythical leap by a priest on horseback in the sixteenth century to escape English forces. To the right is the highest mountain in Cork, Knockboy, which is 706m. To the left in the distance are the MacGillycuddy's Reeks. Behind is Bantry Bay with Whiddy Island an obvious feature. However, this route goes onwards. Or downwards, to be more precise, on a poor, gravelly road, but great to descend after the previous trial. This next section is in County Kerry.

After 3km take the left option at the fork. After another 4km the road swings right before you arrive at a three-way junction after 5km. Go right. By now you are climbing above the Cork-to-Killarney road and there are great views down the valley. The village of Kilgarvan is another 8km farther on.

Leave the village and take the Bantry road. The next 19km, with a gradual climb to the pass of the Borlin Valley and then the sweeping descent on the other side, is one of the great cycling roads in Ireland. The Shehy Mountains rise up like a forbidding wall, streams tumble down, and bundles of fuchsia dangle. A brief road tunnel affords access under a rocky protuberance. Below lies the endlessly brown Slaheny River Bog, which has been undisturbed for millennia. The col appears too quickly. From here it is a bolt down through the opposite valley of 8km and a flat section of 6km back to the car.

29. Youghal and River Blackwater Circuit

Youghal – Cappoquin – Villierstown – Youghal

Location:	Counties Cork and Waterford
Grade:	3
Distance:	50km
Height gain:	608m
Duration:	2.5 to 3 hours
Verdict:	Outstanding

Start/finish

On the Waterford side of Youghal on the N25 there is a small car park on the right, where usually a chip van plies its trade. Park here.

If small is beautiful then this route is the argument clincher. A wonderfully leisurely cycle through the sylvan landscape of east Cork and west Waterford, accompanied by the sonorous River Blackwater for much of the route.

Route description

Within sight of the car park, to the left, is the bridge to Dungarvan. Don't cross it. Instead duck to the left on the L2004 through the woods and the start of a majestic cycle. The route is flanked to the left by an ancient oak forest and the right by the second longest river in the country, the Blackwater, as it winds its way from Youghal through Cappoquin, Lismore, Fermoy and Mallow after rising near the Kerry border. There are occasional glimpses to be had of the eighteenth-century Georgian mansion, Ballynatray House, where avant-garde director Stanley Kubrick filmed *Barry Lyndon* in the 1970s. After 3km, there is a steep climb for a further 3km but thereafter nothing so strenuous.

After levelling off for a while, the road continues through the woods before emerging in some open pastureland and the ugly Camphire Bridge, which straddles the River Bride. Cross over.

Just on from here is a section of the road that runs parallel to the river. There is a great view of Dromina House, a prominent period mansion, on the opposite bank.

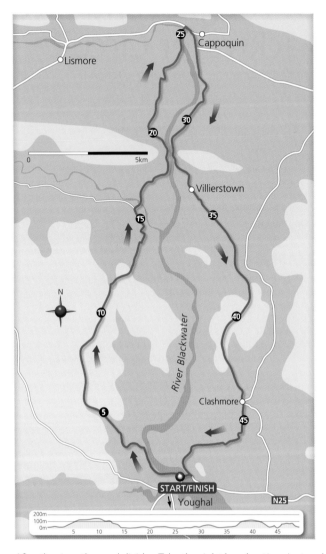

After the river, the road divides. Take the right-hand option. Just under 3km later, on a terrible road surface, bear right and then immediately left. This brings you directly into Cappoquin, a good spot for a coffee – where better than the Railway Bar where former proprietor Jimmy Foley was twice All-Ireland cycling champion?

On leaving the town take the N72 in the direction of Waterford but continue straight after 1km. On the return leg, the River Blackwater is

On the Hindu-style bridge leading to Dromina House near Villierstown, County Waterford

frequently within 500m of the road but is not visible owing to thick vegetation. This section has one of the most jaw-dropping sights in Ireland, the totally unexpected Gothic Hindu bridge that leads into the aforementioned estate of Dromina House. It was constructed for the Villiers-Stuart family on their return from India in the 1820s. For a moment you are in Mogul India with Kipling.

Suitably gobsmacked, the cyclist continues. Villierstown lies 11km distant on reasonable roads. This was the birthplace of the runner John Treacy who won a silver medal in the marathon at the LA Olympic Games in 1984. Continue directly south for the next 10km through the hamlet of Aglish and on to the village of Clashmore. Ignore the first and second left-hand turns and continue straight on south. At the next obvious fork, bear left. After another 2km go left at the crossroads. This brings you onto the N25 at Youghal Bridge. The car is across the bridge to the left.

30. Ross Castle–Black Valley Loop, Kerry

Ross Castle – Killarney – Gap of Dunloe – Black Valley – Moll's Gap – Ross Castle

Location:	County Kerry
Grade:	3
Distance:	60km
Height gain:	757m
Duration:	3 to 3.5 hours
Verdict:	Amazing views: irresistible

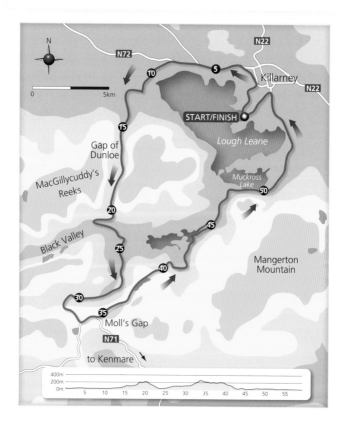

Start/finish

From Killarney town centre, take the N71/Muckross Road and turn right onto the Ross Road. Park at Ross Castle.

Ross Castle, Killarney

While road cycling is wonderful in itself, the prospect of traffic-free roads is a liberating experience. That heightened sense of caution that cyclists have on the roads is assuaged by the guaranteed car-free roads of dedicated cycle tracks. Alas, not all of this route is like that, but a good section of it is. And those bits that are not on cycle paths go through the Black Valley, which is the next best thing.

Route description

Take the path heading northwards from the fifteenth-century Ross Castle. This is the northern section of Killarney National Park and is full of walkers, runners and cyclists complementing the day trippers, photographers, birdwatchers and boat-trippers all around. The path crosses a small bridge – keep an eye out for the rare breed of black Kerry cattle – and continues near the cathedral before veering left. Staying in the woods for another 4km, the track eventually emerges opposite the road to Milltown.

Go left on the N72 main road towards Killorglin, passing through Fossa – childhood home of actor Michael Fassbender. After 2km pick up the road to the Gap of Dunloe, signposted here and at two further junctions. It may be a little early for a break but Kate Kearney's cottage has been a welcoming hostelry for generations of hillwalkers and cyclists. This is a regular start point for hillwalkers taking on the nearby Shehy and Purple Mountains or the longer trek the length of the MacGillycuddy's Reeks to Ireland's highest mountain, Carrauntoohil.

Manoeuvre past any jarveys and continue through the spellbinding Gap of Dunloe, which looks like the land that time forgot. Huge cliffs tower above the road winding ever upwards. Several lakes and bridges complete a magical picture. The road reaches a col and allows great views down into the Black Valley.

Descend carefully into the valley and go left after 2km. The right-hand option continues to the end of the Black Valley from whence hardy walkers emerge on their way to completing the Kerry Way route, which takes in the entire peninsula. Pass a small church and continue on an exceptionally winding road, which leads out of the valley towards Moll's Gap. However, another junction presents itself first. This is to the left, towards Lord Brandon's Cottage from where it is possible to take a boat right back to Ross Castle – and a very interesting way to end this ride if so desired. The fee (at the time of writing) for a cyclist and bike is €13.50.

Passing that option, the next junction appears after 8km. Go left and begin a steep climb to the gap. Only the odd car ventures onto these roads so there is plenty of time to contemplate the majesty of nature.

Moll's Gap is another good spot for a break. Continue north-east towards Killarney on the N71, which thunders down through the western side of the national park, before passing the well-known viewing point of Ladies' View, a boarded-up church, and skirting the lakes, passing Muckross, and finally fetching up at the signposted road that leads back to Ross Castle.

31. Grand Vee Circuit, Waterford

Lismore – Clogheen – Ardfinnan – Clonmel –
Newcastle – Cappoquin – Lismore

Location:	Counties Waterford and Tipperary
Grade:	4/5
Distance:	94km
Height gain:	1,079m
Duration:	5 to 6 hours
Verdict:	Life-affirming

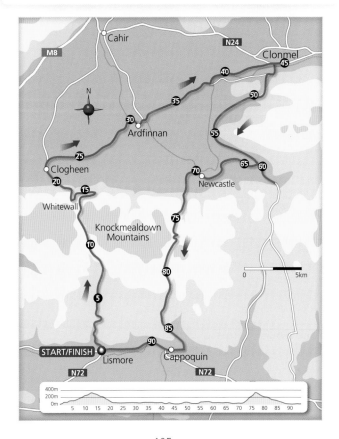

Start/finish

Start in the lovely town of Lismore, County Waterford, on the banks of the River Blackwater. Arriving from the west on the N72, continue left in the direction of Cappoquin. There is a public car park on the left, 100m after the square.

Crossing the bridge in Lismore with Lismore Castle in the background

The Vee is one of the great cycle roads in Ireland, so named for a V-shaped kink in the road. The gradual ascent is none too challenging, just a gentle draw up the western side of the Knockmealdown Mountains. There are not many roads that directly cross Irish mountains near the summits – the Galtees and the MacGillycuddy's Reeks being two of the ranges that do not have traversing roads – so it is great to find one that does, affording elevated views of the valleys. Lismore Castle Gardens are worth a visit: in addition to abundant flora, there are two pieces of the Berlin Wall on display.

Route description

Take the road to Cappoquin, the N72, from Lismore but, once past the castle on the left and across the bridge, go straight ahead on the R668. So begins a gorgeous ascent initially through woods alongside the River Owenashad. This is a category 4/5 climb for 13km but is on the lower end of difficult. By the top of the climb you have passed into Tipperary, if not seventh heaven. Various human memorials decorate the landscape – a commemorative stone to three people killed in an air crash in the 1980s, a Marian shrine and the grave of Samuel Grubb who was buried on Sugarloaf Hill in the 1920s – the Grubb Monument. The Galtees stand dramatically straight ahead and Sugar Loaf Mountain to the right. Farther east are the Comeraghs through which this route returns.

Take a deep breath and begin the charge down the lofty mountain to the peaceful village of Clogheen and swing right onto the R665; now the charge towards Clonmel begins. Along this road is a great view to the right of the Knockmealdowns from whence you blasted. Next up is the pretty village of Ardfinnan on the River Suir. Continue straight through, still on the R665 to Clonmel. The roads are of good quality and you arrive into Clonmel in no time. This is the halfway point and a good spot for a break. At O'Gorman's bakery and cafe there is a wall of posters and paraphernalia dedicated to Irish cycling, including Sean Kelly, and local man and former Irish road race champion Anthony O'Gorman who works there.

After coffee retrace the route for 1km and swing left over the bridge R671 and then straight away go right. This road now has a concave bend for 12km on a very busy road. Grin and bear it. Two kilometres before Ballymacarbry take a right. This is a very rural road and arrives in the village of Newcastle after 6km with no obvious dilemmas.

In the village take the second left. This is the start of a 7km, 9 per cent gradient climb. Tough. Think of the downhill, though! Crossing from Tipperary back into Waterford, blaze a downhill trail for 11km. After 5km you zoom past Mount Melleray before reaching a junction. Go right and right again after 3km and into Cappoquin. From here, amble back to the car, 6km straight ahead on the N72.

Ardfinnan Bridge, County Tipperary

107

32. Comeraghs Circuit, Waterford

*Mahon Bridge (near) – Rathgormack – Ballymacarbry – Kilbrien –
Lemybrien – Kilrossanty – Mahon Bridge (near)*

Location:	County Waterford
Grade:	4
Distance:	70km
Height gain:	1,092m
Duration:	4 to 5 hours
Verdict:	One of the most outstanding descents in Ireland (or Munster, at least)

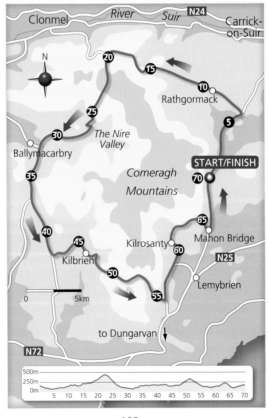

Start/finish

About 8km outside Dungarvan on the N25 road to Waterford the road forks. Take the road to the left, the R676. Nine kilometres up the road park at a forest lay-by on the left.

The Comeraghs are a superb example of glaciated landscape. In their interior, sadly not visible from the road are some of the best examples of corries in Ireland. The Old Red Sandstone was scooped out by the ice, leaving a lake surrounded on three sides by sheer cliffs. Well worth a tramp off the bike – and starting at the same lay-by.

Route description

From the lay-by, take the R676, heading north through open countryside and small woods. The surfaces along here are good and there is minimal traffic. After 6km, the road comes to a crossroads. Turn left.

After 13km of virtually straight roads with some minor rises and falls, turn sharp left onto a tertiary road (watch for the signpost to Hanora's Cottage). This road is in miserable condition with just parts of it passable – but persevere! Climb for about 4km on a really steep incline. By this stage a height of 434m has been reached so the reward of a charging descent is imminent. The landscape is coniferous and deciduous forest, and some open bog. The road is fairly dire but it improves near the bottom. The descent to the village of Ballymacarbry is about 10km and is a death-defying, nerve-wracking blast of a ride, owing to the steepness and condition of the road, which cuts one way, then the next, before swirling through a bridge in a wood – drop to the lowest gear here – before taking off again.

Ballymacarbry is a great spot for a break as it has some nice pubs. Resuming, veer left at the O'Maoloid pub, heading towards Dungarvan. For the next 9km there is an excellent surface. After 9km swing hard left on the signposted road to Kilbrien. This is due east and, after passing through the village, head south-east on pretty good roads for 12km before intersecting a T-junction. Go left (north) and shortly pass through the village of Kilrossanty. This road briefly turns in towards the mountains before arcing away due east. A turn to the left is for the popular Mahon Falls. Ignore it, continuing on as the road curves to Mahon Bridge. The start/finish point is 4km to the left.

33. Glenbeigh–Caragh Lake Return, Kerry

Glenbeigh – Caragh Lake – Killorglin – Glenbeigh

Location:	County Kerry
Grade:	2
Distance:	50km
Height gain:	516m
Duration:	2.5 to 3 hours
Verdict:	Magnificent Caragh Lake is the companion for much of this trip. Very quiet roads.

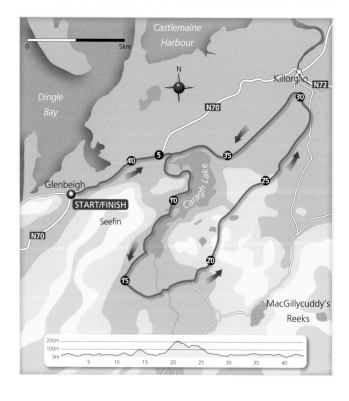

Start/finish

Begin in the pretty seaside village of Glenbeigh, situated on the north side of the Iveragh Peninsula, 35km from Killarney. There is ample parking on the main street.

The famous Ring of Kerry cycle passes through here, if you fancy doing that some time – 171km of pleasure! In the summer the beach at Rossbeigh echoes to the thud of horses' hooves as they are raced up and down the beach.

Route description

Head towards Killarney on the N70 and cross over a small bridge (which can accommodate only single-lane car traffic). Across the bridge resist the temptation to cycle left into what was recently described as one of Europe's fifty hidden gems by the Lonely Planet – Cromane Peninsula.

Just up the road after a popular scenic viewing point for tourists of the surrounding mountains, turn right and descend briefly into a valley before ascending the side of an imposing hill. Emerging at the glorious lake front early in the morning as the mist sweeps across the water is a transcendent moment. Caragh Lake is a famous fishery and at various points along the road anglers are readying themselves for their forthcoming tussle with trout.

The road briefly turns south-east before turning again north-east to Blackstones Bridge, which crosses the River Caragh. Though just 20km into this cycle the wood at Lickeen cries out to be visited. A beautiful riverside walk beside the River Caragh is well worth this diversion. In summer, electric-blue and green damselflies proliferate.

Remount and cycle the 12km north-east to the outskirts of Killorglin. Along the way, some superb scenery unfolds of upland peat, yellow-brown in the late summer sun.

Having arrived at the edge of Killorglin, famous for Puck Fair, where a goat is crowned king for the duration of the three-day festival, held every August, turn sharp left and head south-west on a route roughly parallel to the one from Caragh Lake. This is the Farrantoreen Road. It soon arrives at the northern shores of Caragh Lake and the tree-lined avenues afford occasional glimpses of the lake past some handsome houses. Soon it reconnects with the main road, the N70, which leads back in a few short kilometres to Glenbeigh.

34. Cahersiveen–Valentia Circuit, Kerry

Cahersiveen – Portmagee – Knight's Town – Portmagee –
St Finan's Bay – Ballinskelligs Bay – Cahersiveen

Location:	County Kerry
Grade:	4
Distance:	66km
Height gain:	824m
Duration:	4 hours
Verdict:	Sublime views: irresistible

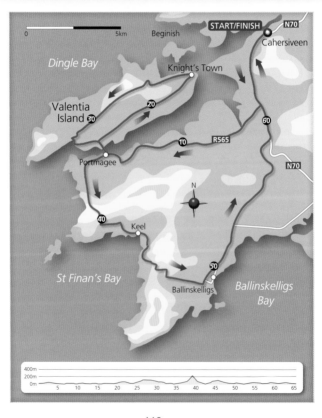

Start/finish

Cahersiveen. Park on the Waterville side.

The Ring of Kerry cycle would just be too long if it were to take in all the roads on this route but some offer tremendous views and must be included. This is one of the best (if not *the* best) routes in this book. A car ferry links from Reenard Point outside Cahersiveen to Knight's Town on Valentia. Just up the road, following the signposts, is the extraordinary evidence of a creature called a tetrapod that crawled out of the sea 385 million years ago and left a trail of footprints, now fossilised.

Route description

Head south-west from Cahersiveen towards Waterville on the N70. After 5km the quality of road surface deteriorates on swinging right towards Portmagee on the R565. This takes the rider across a bog with Canuig Mountain on Bolus Head visible off to the left. On the right is Portmagee Channel separating the mainland from Valentia Island. After 11km the bridge to the island appears. The bridge was built in 1970, providing a much-needed link to the mainland, but compromising Valentia's island status.

Valentia Island Lighthouse on the road from Knight's Town to the west of the island.

Cross the bridge and turn right on the R565 towards Knight's Town at the eastern tip of the island. Along the way is the second village on the island: Chapeltown. From mid July to September, Valentia Island turns orange with colonies of montbretia decorating the hedges. Knight's Town is a fine spot for a break, with some nice cafes and pubs. The pier is a hive of activity with pleasure boats coming and going and children learning how to sail.

Back on board the bike, take the right-hand road climbing out of the village. Soon you come to an arboreal oasis. A tree-tunnel of birch, ash, sycamore and holly surrounds the cyclist. Valentia Island Lighthouse can be glimpsed through the trees. At the first junction, it is well worth taking the middle road to the Slate Quarry from where the views are awe-inspiring. In the distance lie the Blasket Islands and Slea Head on the Dingle Peninsula. Cycle back down to the road: Valentia Harbour and the wondrously shaped Beginish Island lie ahead.

Back at the junction, go right and right again. After 6km the road turns south, then east, back towards the bridge to complete the circum-navigation of Valentia. The Skellig Islands loom out at sea like twin pyramids. Cross the bridge into Portmagee and turn right through the village and follow the signs for Ballinskelligs. After 2km take a big gulp. Another 2km ahead lies one of the toughest hills in the country. Known as the Skellig Ring, the road has a 9 per cent gradient followed by one of 14 per cent. Added to that, the surface is poor. It can be knocked off in stages, however: a flat stretch, a bend, an area to pull in, allowing traffic to pass.

Struggle to the top somehow and then marvel at the views. The restless eye does not know where to look. Descend slowly, for there are many bends, into St Finan's Bay and then take the coast road to Ballinskelligs on a fine climb to the col and another great descent on the other side. From Ballinskelligs, continue on the R566, straight for 8km, and then crookedly for 2km until intersecting the N70 again. Cahersiveen lies 6km to the left.

35. Glandore–Baltimore Loop, Cork

Glandore – Union Hall – Castletownshend – Tragumna – Lough Ine –
Baltimore – Oldcourt – Skibbereen – Drinagh – Leap – Glandore

Location:	County Cork
Grade:	4
Distance:	83km
Height gain:	1,050m
Duration:	5 to 6 hours
Verdict:	Magnificent coastal route past cliffs and crashing waves.

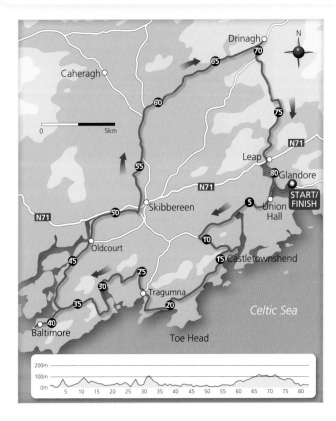

Start/finish

The start point is the village of Glandore, 4km south of the N71 at Leap.

Cyclists who like a flat chase along say, twenty Carrigrohane Straights, should opt out of this route. It has over 1,000 metres of climbing on often very poor roads. The upside is some very good roads and some of the glorious scenery for which west Cork is famous, and many attractive towns and villages along the way.

The bridge between Glandore and Union Hall

Route description

Descending through Glandore follow the excellent R597 north until reaching a bridge after 2km. Cross it and continue on to the beautiful fishing village of Union Hall. From here to Baltimore, 30km distant, the route for the most part hugs the coast. Continue through the village and a tough-ish winding climb till the road descends gradually towards the tiny village of Rinneen. Press on to a crossroads and take the left turn for Castletownshend – an old Protestant ascendancy village whose character is markedly different from the vernacular 'Catholic' towns and villages in the area. A great downhill charge past one of Ireland's few remaining public phone boxes and an impressive beech tree in the middle of the road brings you to the water's edge. St Barrahane's Church has stained-glass windows by artist Harry Clarke.

Turn and cycle back up the hill. Watch out for a signpost to the left for

Castletownshend, County Cork

Toe Head. Take it. A lovely, twisting road with great views brings you to the wild cliffs of Toe Head and on to Tragumna. A sandy beach here is an enticing spot for a swim in summer.

The next section to Lough Ine is tricky. Climb the hill out of Tragumna – above the beach. Continue for just under 2km and then take a sharp left turn – due west. Cycle along this road for just under 2km and then take a sharp right. Climb for a few hundred metres and take the second left. After 2km, go right at the crossroads and then take the second left. This road rises for a bit before descending dramatically, with the forested hill of Knockomagh ahead. The route intersects the main Lough Ine-to-Skibbereen road here, and Lough Ine itself is 200m to the left. Take a break – there is a pier a few hundred metres to the left – and marvel at one of only three saltwater lakes in the country, which is home to a wealth of marine life unique to Ireland.

Back on the bike, turn left at the entrance to the wood – a must-do walk for another day. After 100m take the left-hand option. This road is one of the most gorgeous in the country: towering beeches and oak surround you while, below, the turquoise waters of the lake sparkle. After 2km of this terrific stretch the road veers right and climbs for 1.5km, on a poor surface. At the summit of this road dismount to look behind at the mighty Atlantic, or in front at the myriad islands scattered across Roaringwater Bay like rare minerals. After a few hundred metres is a T-junction. Turn left (onto a diabolical road). This intersects the R595 and goes directly to Baltimore. Time for a well-earned break. No better spot for a sandwich than Bushe's bar overlooking the pier.

Fully rested and back on the bike, take the R595 north towards Skibbereen. At Oldcourt go straight on, on a lovely quiet road above the River Ilen to Skibbereen. On entering the town take the left-hand option, pass the West Cork Hotel and at the roundabout take the third exit (onto the Marsh road).

After 2km turn right across Ballyhilty Bridge and then go left at the fork. Push on for just under 1km till you intersect the R593 and go left. Stay on this road for 3.5km before taking a right-hand turn onto the L4231 for Drinagh, 9km distant. Make a sharp right in the village onto the R637, which you leave almost immediately on the left-hand fork. After 500m, turn right. Cycle for just under 4km, then turn right at Corran Lake (out of view). Leap is 3km from here with Glandore a further 3km. Stunning.

36. Cashel Circuit, Tipperary

Cashel – Dundrum – Tipperary – Bansha – New Inn – Cashel

Location:	County Tipperary
Grade:	3
Distance:	65km
Height gain:	429m
Duration:	3 to 3.5 hours
Verdict:	Wonderful woods and quiet roads

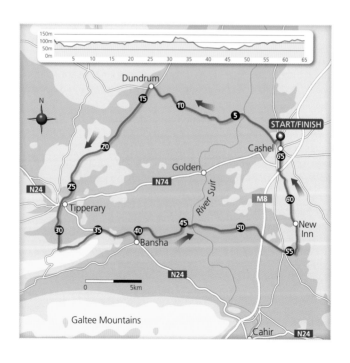

Start/finish

Start at the north side of Cashel on the Horse and Jockey road, the R639. There is ample parking near the Esso garage on Ladyswell Street.

Near New Inn, County Tipperary

The pretty Tipperary village of Golden is the centre of this route, although the route does not pass through it on account of the extremely truck-dense N74 which links Tipperary to Cashel, as this writer discovered on a recce for this cycle. The N74 is described as the Bianconi Drive after the Italian who set up a horse-drawn carriage route here in the early nineteenth century. However, the only allure is in the name.

Route description

Take the road to the left of the Esso garage, the R660. After 200m go left, passing under the world-famous Rock of Cashel, and after 300m go right, onto the R505. This is a lovely road that passes through some of the rustic splendours of north Tipperary: rolling countryside, abundant streams, ponds, woods and lots of peace and quiet. After 4km cross Camus Bridge over the River Suir before the road veers left by 90 degrees. From here it is 10km to the appealing wooded hamlet of Dundrum, home to a fine country house hotel of the same name.

At a T-Junction in Dundrum take a sharp left and go left again at a fork. This is the R661 to Tipperary town. If you're lucky enough to cycle this on a rainy day in spring, revel in the drenched tree tunnels and intoxicating aromas of spring flowers. Tipperary is 1km distant on a pleasant south-westerly route. Take a break in the town – Brazil's cafe on the main street has a small courtyard where you can put the bike.

Near the cafe is Castle Street and the start of the R664. Go down this road for 3.5km to a T-Junction. Go left on what's known locally as the Mountain Road (L8214) and enjoy a great 4km stretch of woods. Thereafter the fun is over as the route necessitates a 4km section on the busy N24 connecting Tipperary to Cahir. Go right, stay in close to the ditch and grin and bear it.

Next up is the graceful village of Bansha. A fine spot for a picnic on the banks of the River Ara. At the start of the village is a road to the left. This goes northwards for 1km and through a level crossing before turning east at a small racetrack. Stay on this road for 4m to reach a T-junction. Go left for under 1km before turning right. This road runs in a straight line for 6.5km before arriving at a T-junction. Go right. New Inn appears after 3km. Continue straight through the junction; bear left for 1km before turning sharp left, north after 1km at the sign for St Declan's Way. This is a lovely, quiet country road that leads directly to Cashel after 10km.

Approaching the town, pass the first roundabout and take the first left at the next. Continue straight to the town square and then right up the hill to return to the starting point.

37. Circuit of the Reeks, Kerry

Killarney – Beaufort – Ballaghbeama Pass –
Killarney National Park – Beaufort – Killarney

Location:	County Kerry
Grade:	4
Distance:	86km
Height gain:	1,198m
Duration:	5 to 6 hours
Verdict:	Remote mountain pass, with zero traffic in places

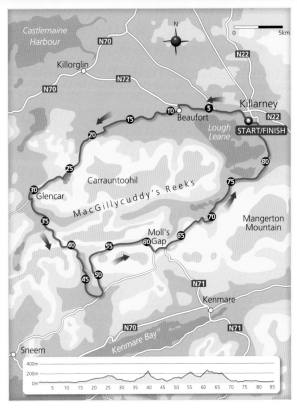

Start/finish

Start by the cathedral in Killarney on the R877. There is usually enough parking nearby.

Bridge at Beaufort, County Kerry

This cycle takes you over one of the highest mountain passes in the country but curiously it is not a difficult climb as you have ascended gradually by the time you get to the last drag. Like Mount Brandon on the Dingle Peninsula, which is always swathed in mist, so too is Ballaghbeama.

Route description

Heading west out of Killarney on the R877, look for signs for Killorglin and the N72. The traffic is pretty busy here for a while and there is just a small bicycle lane to offer protection. Ignore the first turn, which goes to the Gap of Dunloe. Soon the road widens and after a few kilometres there is a turn-off to the left for Beaufort. Admire the arched bridge, if you're so inclined. Arriving in the charming village of Beaufort – a beautiful name, but the

Irish one, *Lios an Phúca,* is much more evocative, the fort of the ghosts – immediately take a sharp right.

Just along the road here is a remarkable example of Ogham stonework – the fourth-century runic inscriptions carved onto standing stones. These ones have been gathered from several derelict sites. This road is quiet and in pretty good condition. It affords a great view of the Gap of Dunloe and, farther along, of Ireland's highest mountain, Carrauntoohil, which stands 1,039m high.

Continue along this road, passing several start points for the ascent of Carrauntoohil: the Gap of Dunloe itself, Cronin's Yard, Lislebane, the Hydro Road and lastly Lough Acoose. Continue on to the Climbers Inn at Glencar, which is a good spot for a break. After another 1.5km, at a T-junction turn sharp left for Ballaghbeama. At the next fork go right (straight ahead is a dead end) and so on to Ballaghbeama and the imposing mountain of Mullaghanattin glaring down.

This is a really wonderful, remote place. As you snake through the bends on the approach with towering cliffs above, you realise this is what cycling is all about. Take a brief rest at the col before a spellbinding descent through bogland, past woods and streams and on to a junction. Go left, then take another left almost immediately. After 5km, pass a small road to the left and almost straight away, take the right-hand option at a fork. This keeps you away from the lakeshore. Pass lovely Lough Brin below to your left nestled under the foreboding Knockaunanattin Mountain. The shabby road climbs to a col before a fine descent. After 7km on the road from the lake, the road turns sharply right. Take it and climb to the main road and turn left for Moll's Gap. A fantastic road lies before you. By now into the upper fringes of Killarney National Park, the road has more turns and twists than a Raymond Chandler novel. Regretfully it ends after 10km, but with the soul recalibrated, charge along the final 10km on the shores of the lake, back to the car.

38. Sheep's Head Peninsula Loop

Bantry – Durrus – Ahakista – Kilcrohane –
Sheep's Head – Bantry

Location:	County Cork
Grade:	3
Distance:	67km
Height gain:	751m
Duration:	3 to 3.5 hours
Verdict:	A superb cycle on a sunny day, but surprisingly hilly

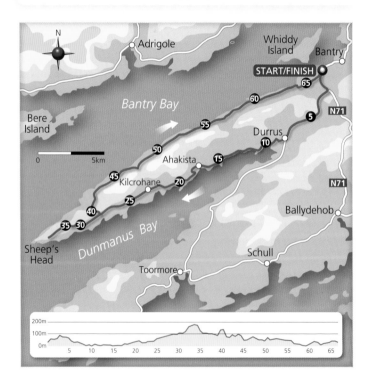

Start/finish

Start on the west side of Bantry on the N71 to Skibbereen. Park at the Westlodge Hotel – this is as good a place as any to begin.

This is probably the most peaceful and traffic-free cycle in the guide and offers breathtaking views of the Mizen Peninsula on the outward journey and the Beara Peninsula on the return leg. The cycling is carefree, though with plenty of small hills. The clifftop lighthouse is the halfway mark on the route, should you decide to walk the final 2km to reach it. No road winds there but it is well worth the tramp.

Route description

From the start point, continue south on the N71 Skibbereen road but after 1.5km peel off to the right and onto the R591. The road is of good quality and rapidly brings you to the quiet village of Durrus.

Continue through the village and take the right-hand option when the road forks. (The left-hand option goes to Mizen Head.) With the sea constantly ahead it feels almost like cycling on a ship's deck. Dunmanus Bay is a relatively quiet bay for fishing as there are no towns or villages directly on the coast owing to the mountainous topography.

Next up is the tiny village of Ahakista, which will forever be linked with the Air India crash of 1985 in which 329 people died. There is a poignant memorial to them by the sea.

On the road to Ahakista on the Sheep's Head Peninsula

The roads on this route are generally quiet. That is partly a reflection on the land quality, much of which is poor and therefore less likely to support a farming community. Next up is the hamlet of Kilcrohane, a start point for some of the walking routes on the peninsula.

From Kilcrohane it is another 11km to the end of the road at a cafe – and a good spot for a break. There are fantastic views south to the Mizen Head. However, if you walk the further 2km out to the end of the peninsula, the views from the lighthouse are greater still. In the distance is Dursey Island – which has Ireland's only cable car link to an island. Directly across the bay is Bere Island, one of the biggest islands in the country. At the lighthouse you can even indulge in some whale watching as several species, including minke, fin and humpback, sometimes pass within view.

Back on the bike after the break and retrace the route in an eastwards direction. After 5.5km take a sharp left. The road turns back somewhat before winding onto the north side of the peninsula. This has to be one of the quietest roads in the country. If you're lucky, you may witness the spectacle of gannets diving into the sea at speeds of up to 100km/h in search of fish. The roads here are frequently in diabolical condition but not enough to stop you getting through. With Bantry Bay on the left and mountains of purple heather and orange gorse on the right, the road goes right back to the car. There are no villages or towns from here, just you and your bike. Near the end of the cycle the road forks: go right, (left also returns to the start). One final point of interest is just before the end where you can see the huge oil storage tanks on Whiddy Island, which is the Irish oil reserve.

39. Millstreet–Gneevgullia Return, Cork

Millstreet – Gneevgullia – Knocknagree – Millstreet

Location:	County Cork
Grade:	3
Distance:	48km
Height gain:	569m
Duration:	3 to 3.5 hours
Verdict:	Mountain-hugging and fresh air

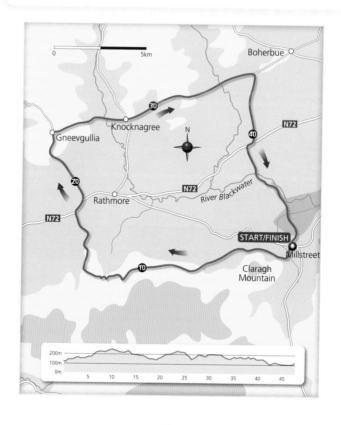

Start/finish

Millstreet, County Cork. Park at the west end of the town.

This is a rural cycle in north-west Cork and is one of the most car-free routes in the guide. The route is a rough parallelogram. Millstreet's claim to fame is that it hosted the Eurovision song contest in 1993.

Route description

Take the Claragh Road, which is to the right of the church. (Avoid at all costs the hectic R582 to Rathmore.) Cross the River Finnow and after 1km from the church the road swings right and traverses beneath an imposing facade of mountains: Claragh Mountain, Caherbarnagh and the Paps. Several noticeboards from the rural development company IRD Duhallow inform the walker or cyclist of the flora and fauna of the region, including the delightful wheatear.

This road has a gradual climb and continues along just under the mountains for 13km. After 12km the road crosses the signposted border into Kerry.

By now the foothills of the gently contoured Paps have appeared. The hills are a favourite with hillwalkers but from the other side – the Clydagh Valley just off the Cork-to-Killarney road. The breast-shaped mountains are named for the mother of the Irish gods, Danú.

Near Gneevgullia, County Kerry

After another 2km from the border swing right, heading north – the second side of the parallelogram. Pass a considerable bog on the right and arrive at a T-junction. Skirt briefly to the left and then right after 100m and the road passes Rathmore GAA pitch. Veering right, the road connects to the N72 Mallow-to-Killarney road.

Head right, or east, briefly. In just under 1km follow the signs to, for some, the unpronounceable, Gneevgullia. A toughish climb leads into the village. The village has a widespread reputation that belies its size, being the focal point for the Irish traditional Sliabh Luachra musical style. It is also the birthplace of the renowned seanchaí Eamon Kelly, a statue of whom adorns the main street. It is a good spot to stop for refreshments.

Back on the bike and swing right (from the earlier approach) towards the next village, Knocknagree, on largely good roads. This is the third side of the parallelogram. Cross the mighty Blackwater River after 3km. The river rises about 10km north of this point at Knockanefune and for a stretch of around 20km forms the Kerry/Cork border. Push on to the spacious village of Knocknagree and depart to the east on the L1108 in the direction of Boherboy. Cross the Owentaraglin River, a tributary of the Blackwater and 2km thereafter head right at a T-junction. This is the final side of the parallelogram.

A pleasant cycle of 4km intersects the N72, which has to be briefly taken on. Go right on this seeming motorway before sanctuary presents itself across the road in the shape of the road for base. Millstreet lies 7km farther along on a largely characterless road, save for the railway crossing 1km from the town.

40. East Clare Circuit

Ballina/Killaloe – Broadford – Bridgetown – Killaloe/Ballina

Location:	Counties Tipperary and Clare
Grade:	2
Distance:	45km
Height gain:	293m
Duration:	2 to 3 hours
Verdict:	Serene exploration of Lough Derg and environs

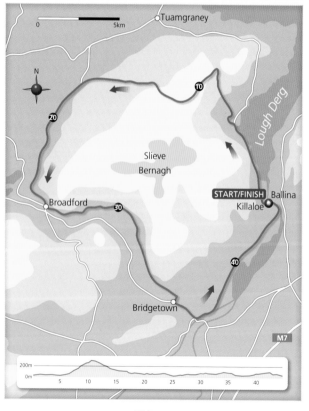

Start/finish

Park in the 'dual' settlement of Ballina (County Tipperary) and Killaloe (County Clare), which lie on either side of the River Shannon linked by a thirteen-arch bridge. There is pay parking along the lakeside.

Bridge across the River Shannon at Killaloe

This route affords fine views of Lough Derg, the second largest lake in the Republic (after Lough Corrib). It is 130 square kilometres and has shores on Clare, Galway and Tipperary. It has numerous islands, including Holy Island, complete with the Early Christian abbey and round tower. The departure point for excursions to Holy Island is Mountshannon, from which can be seen Eagle Island, where white-tailed eagles settled in 2011 following the introduction programme in Killarney National Park in 2007. This route is not suitable for racers.

Route description

Cross the bridge from Ballina and turn right onto the R463. The popularity of the place is obvious from the number of pleasure cruisers on the river. Along the road there are several viewing points for Lough Derg.

Branch off to the left after 5km in the direction of the Piper's Inn. A long climb of 4km ensues on virtually traffic-free roads. The bowl-like valley now falls below the road giving wonderful views of Lough Derg. Go left at a church. The road briefly curves southwards before climbing gently past a forested area and arriving at a bog at the summit of Slieve Bernagh.

The reason for not bringing a racer becomes obvious over the next 5km became the road disintegrates into gravel and potholes. Bear with it and enjoy the views northwards across the bogs to the Slieve Aughty Mountains in the north of the county. Eventually, the road intersects the R465. Go left (south) towards the village of Broadford.

This was a historic crossing point for people travelling through the Slieve Bernagh range towards Limerick. The nearby Doon Lake once lapped the shores of the village until a drainage scheme at Sixmilebridge saw the waters retreat. The inventor of the submarine, J. P. Holland, lived for a time at the lake.

In the village take a small road to the left (prior to crossing the bridge) in the direction of the townland of Kilbane. After 4km heading east, the road veers southwards. This is a gorgeous road with interleaving valleys creating pockets of rich farmland. Continue through to Bridgetown and onwards till intersecting the R463. This is a busy road but is quite wide and has a great surface for the most part. Killaloe is 8km to the left (north) where the start point of Ballina lies across the bridge.

On the approach to Killaloe, the impressive St Flannan's Cathedral can be seen. The town was the birthplace of Brian Boru in the tenth century and was later his seat of power as it was a vital crossing point on the River Shannon.

The author above Lough Derg, County Clare

41. Loop North from Cork City

Cork – Glanmire – Leamlara – Lisgoold – Midleton – Ballynoe – Conna – Rathcormac – Glenville – Cork

Location:	County Cork
Grade:	4/5
Distance:	106km
Height gain:	1,142m
Duration:	4.5 to 5.5 hours
Verdict:	Terrific rolling countryside on good roads

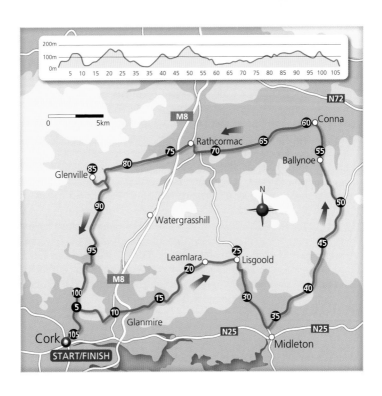

Start/finish

Cork city. Start at Patrick's Bridge. There are several public car parks in the vicinity.

For lovers of hamlets there are plentiful examples on this route – Leamlara, Ballynoe, Aghern. For lovers of *Hamlet*, there is even an estate in Midleton called Elsinore. To cycle or not to cycle? The former, of course! Beautiful countryside, winding rivers, thickets of woods and kilometre after kilometre of quiet and relatively quiet country roads.

Route description

From Patrick's Bridge, traverse MacCurtain Street. At the third set of traffic lights, climb up Summerhill South to the left and on to Dillon's Cross. Continue through a busy junction onto Ballyhooly Road. After 4km turn right uphill and head into the countryside. Pass Rathcooney cemetery and turn right. After just under 2km go left. At the first fork in the road go left again, before plunging into the village of Glanmire, beautifully nestled in the woods at the Glashaboy River.

Continue through the junction. After 2km bear right and pass under the M8 motorway. Along the way from Glanmire wild roses throng the hedgerows as does intoxicating honeysuckle. Continue on the winding L3010. Nine kilometres from Glanmire, go right at a fork. Arrive at Leamlara, a crossroads with a church, and continue straight through. For a while the tree canopy thins out and you can see magnificent rolling hills with farmhouses dotted around.

Continue downwards, upwards and onwards to the comparatively populous village of Lisgoold and a sharp right turn onto the main road, the R626. It has a lovely surface and most of it is accompanied by the gurgling Owenacurra River all the way to Midleton, 9km distant. Continue to the town centre with its many fine buildings and turn left on the main street onto the R627. This leads to the village of Dungourney after 9km on excellent, relatively quiet roads. Pass through the village in the direction of Tallow. Pass Leahy's open farm, twisting, dipping and thrusting like a fencer's épée. Seven kilometres from Dungourney, go left at Murley's Cross. Pass through Ballynoe and press on, taking a right-hand turn at the end of the village. Conna looms large and is a welcome break. The castle here was built in 1551 by the FitzGeralds, earls of Desmond, before falling into the hands of Walter Raleigh.

The main purpose in devising this particular route was to take in the gorgeous 14km ribbon of smooth tarmac that leads to Rathcormac. The demand on the legs is minimal and the rider is in cruise control. A T-junction presents itself after 12km – go right. This leads to the outskirts of Rathcormac on the main Cork road, the R639. Go right and head into the village. A sharp left after 1km lines up to the next leg, the R614, to Glenville, 14km distant. Bear left after 9.5km, and then right after 1km to get to Glenville – one of the most charming villages in the country, with its swaying sycamores, a lovely old stone church and a fine old pub, Essy Cuffe's. Retrace the route for 2.5km and go right at the T-Junction, picking up the R614 from earlier. Continue southwards towards Cork on a rising climb back to the summit overlooking the city and then a fantastic cascade to the start point through White's Cross.

Leaving White's Cross, continue straight on the R614 on the Ballyhooly Road, which leads through Ballyvolane to St Luke's Cross on the same road as the one on which you left the city. Continue downhill on Summerhill North to the River Lee where the start/finish point is just to the right along St Patrick's Quay.

42. Carrigrohane–Kanturk Return, Cork

*Carrigrohane – Nad – Banteer – Kanturk – Lombardstown –
Glantane – Bweeng – New Tipperary – Blarney – Carrigrohane*

Location:	County Cork
Grade:	5
Distance:	104km
Height gain:	919m
Duration:	5 to 6 hours
Verdict:	A fine tester for those wishing to step above 100km on good country roads

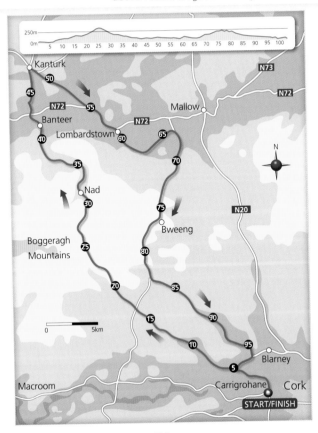

Start/finish

The start point is at the Angler's Rest pub on the west of Cork city in Carrigrohane. Park in the vicinity of the pub.

This route takes in Kanturk, with its seventeenth-century castle. A mighty construction with many fine features, it was never completed on the orders of Crown forces worried that it could become a focal point for rebellion. The town is built at the confluence of two tributaries of the Blackwater: the Allow and Dallow.

Route description

From the Angler's Rest, turn north-west, away from Cork city. At the junction take the R579 in the direction of Blarney. This is a very busy, poorly surfaced road parallel to the River Shournagh, a tributary of the Lee. After 4km much of the traffic turns off this heavily wooded road right towards Blarney. After another 4km a bridge with hanging baskets to the left entices the rider to the village of Berrings. Ignore it and continue on straight.

This stretch of road is virtually a straight line for 30km but with enough character and small bends to give variation. It rises all the time to the village of Nad – 330m in 30km, a fairly gentle rise. Here the contours of the Boggeragh Mountains are gracefully outlined and make for wonderful views, whether shrouded in mist or basking in sunshine. Though there follows a descent of 250m in the next 24km, it is as moderate as the climb.

The road now bends and twists to the railway village of Banteer. Continue straight through to the town of Kanturk whose impressive buildings and quaint park are appealing to the eye, and which is a fine spot for a break.

Back on the bike, take the R576 towards Mallow. Briefly intersect the hellish N72 for 3.5km before taking a right for Lombardstown on the L1212. Cross the Mallow-to-Killarney railway at a level crossing. The road rises gently through Lombardstown and some scattered housing and continues south-eastwards. Pass through another tiny village: Glantane. After that, at the first obvious junction, continue left for another 3km (cross the railway again at another level crossing) till intersecting the busier R619. Go right.

Continue south on good roads. The village of Bweeng is next along before you descend for 20km almost to the finish. After 7km comes the village of New Tipperary as the road divides. Leave the R619 and continue straight rather than turning right. This is the Shournagh Road, a beautiful, quiet country road with a fairly good surface, which goes all the way to Blarney. At the T-Junction 13km from New Tipperary, go right for 1km to another T-junction. Now go right, then left almost immediately. This intersects the R579 and the start/finish point is 4km to the left.

43. Ring of Kerry Challenge

Killarney – Killorglin – Glenbeigh – Cahersiveen – Waterville – Caherdaniel – Castlecove – Sneem – Kenmare – Moll's Gap – Killarney

Location:	County Kerry
Grade:	5
Distance:	171km
Height gain:	1,759m
Duration:	7 to 10 hours
Verdict:	Amazing

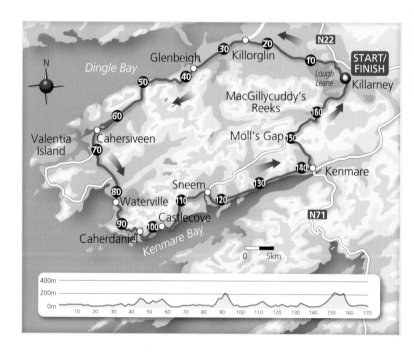

Start/finish

A good place to start is at the free car park on the Muckross Road, 3km south of Killarney. A number of jarveys use the same car park. The benefit of this is made plain when you finish and don't have to compete with Killarney traffic.

At Coomakista, County Kerry

At first sight this is a daunting prospect. There are 171km of roads to cycle and a total ascent of 1,759m. However, break it down into its constituent parts and it is less daunting: Killarney to Glenbeigh 35km; another 25km to Cahersiveen; another 30km to Caherdaniel; 20km more to Sneem; another 25km to Kenmare; another 10km to Moll's Gap; and the last 25km to the finish. Suffice to say there are much shorter routes in this guide that are tougher.

Route description

Take a deep breath and mount up. Cycle into Killarney and go left just after the mini-roundabout. Follow this road for 1.5km and go left again. This is the N70 and is the road you follow for the next 137km until you pick up the N71 at Kenmare. Follow the signs for Killorglin.

A cycle lane affords a modicum of protection from the heavy traffic in this area – assuming you're not doing this as part of the charity cycle, in which case the road will be closed to traffic. By now, the MacGillycuddy's Reeks are in view, including the majestic Carrauntoohil at 1,039m. The road to Killorglin is straightforward and variously of poor and good quality. High hedges limit the views.

At Killorglin you are greeted with a statue of King Puck, the eponymous hero of the town's annual festival, Puck Fair. Cross the bridge into the attractive village, climb the hill and go left to Glenbeigh. By now, the views have started to open up and the mountains of the Dingle Peninsula to the right announce themselves mistily. The road to Glenbeigh again is great in parts and poor in others. Approaching Glenbeigh, cross a bridge over the River Caragh, which drains the Alpine-like Caragh Lake over the mountains to the left.

Enter the pretty village of Glenbeigh and continue through to one of the great cycling roads in the country. As the road climbs slightly, the magnificent views over Dingle Bay come into sight. The road sweeps onwards and downwards into Cahersiveen, birthplace of the Liberator, Daniel O'Connell. Take a break here or just a bit farther on at Waterville – made famous by Charlie Chaplin who used to holiday there. Leave Waterville under the watchful eye of Cahernageeha Mountain as the road rises on a long curve towards Coomakista Pass. Take a mini-break here to marvel at the views: below are Scariff and Deenish Islands, and Dursey Island at the tip of the Beara Peninsula which, like a farmer, minds the Bull, the Cow and the Calf islands farther out.

Charge down the hill into Caherdaniel and on to Castlecove and, if well rested, strike on to Sneem, 15km from Castlecove. A draining, badly surfaced bog road before Sneem is quite a challenge. From Sneem it is 14km on very good roads to the peaceful Blackwater Bridge and another 13km effectively downhill to Kenmare. Take another deserved break here. There are several great cafes and bars in the town. By this stage 80 per cent of the cycle has been achieved. The climb to Moll's Gap from Kenmare is on a regular gradient but on an appalling surface for 4km.

Take another mini-break at Moll's Gap for the wonderful views of the Beara Peninsula. There follows a high road for about 4km before a stupendous downhill cycle through Killarney National Park, with lakes, trees and dappled sunlight just a blur. The road eventually levels off and 10km farther on, return to the car. Congratulations. You've done it!

44. Charleville to the Coast Loop

Charleville – Bruree – Ballingarry – Askeaton – Foynes –
Shanagolden – Ardagh – Newcastle West – Dromcolliher – Milford
– Newtownshandrum – Charleville

Location:	Counties Cork and Limerick
Grade:	5
Distance:	112km
Height gain:	621m
Duration:	5.5 to 6.5 hours
Verdict:	Many towns and villages to discover; some very long, straight roads

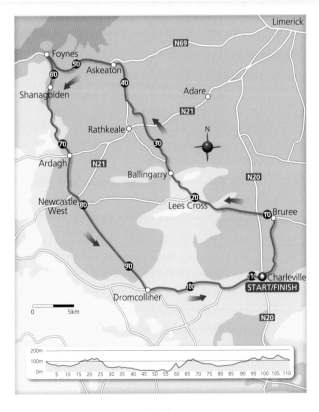

Start/finish

Charleville, County Cork. There is parking on the main street.

Bruree, County Limerick

Limerick is often overlooked for cycling but don't let a dearth of bicycles on the roads put you off. This cycle explores the roads and towns of mid-Limerick and earns its ranking in the top set by virtue of some long, tough roads. But there are several positives: if you're interested in flat cycling, this route presents only 621m climbing over 111km, which is none too onerous considering the Valentia route, for instance, has 823m climbing in 66km; and there is an abundance of towns and villages with which to acquaint yourself.

Route description

From Charleville's main street, take the R515 towards Kilmallock. After 1.5km take a left turn – you are already in Limerick. This is a beautiful winding road, which fetches up in the alluring village of Bruree after 8km. Keep an eye out for the impressive restored mill with a gigantic wheel on the River Maigue.

Leave Bruree east on the R518 towards the next village, Ballingarry. The roads are not inspiring but are relatively quiet. Some 1.5km after Ballingarry, leave the R518 by taking the minor road directly opposite. This veers left straight away and picks up the R518 again after 10km. Next port of call is Askeaton with its impressive twelfth-century Desmond castle standing on a rocky outcrop in the River Deel. Pick up the national secondary route, the

N69, heading for Foynes. It is a very busy road but there is good space in the margin and Foynes lies just 12km distant. The town has a fascinating history, being the former centre of Ireland's fleet of flying boats. A museum showcases one of the planes as well as multiple related artefacts. The Yankee Clipper bar is a fine place to stop for a coffee.

After refreshments retrace the route for 1km and branch off to the right on the R521. First up is the village of Shanagolden, followed by Ardagh. The road is fairly nondescript, the main characteristic being a series of undulations over the low-lying hills. Fairly soon the road arrives in the thriving town of Newcastle West on the River Arra. It is the second biggest town in the county. The imposing twelfth-century FitzGerald castle dominates the town centre and many fine buildings make for an impressive streetscape. The poet Michael Hartnett was born here.

All the perversions of the soul
I learnt on a small farm
… a little music on the road,
a little peace in decrepit stables.

Continue through the town and look for the R522 to Dromcolliher. Any flat-road enthusiasts will love this 16km stretch but it is somewhat monotonous. At the village, turn left on the R515 towards Milford, pass through Newtownshandrum on decent roads and then the final 6km to the start/finish point.

45. Beara Peninsula Circuit

Kenmare–Glengarriff–Adrigole–Castletownbere–Lamb's Head–Allihies – Eyeries – Ardgroom – Lauragh – Kenmare

Location:	Counties Kerry and Cork
Grade:	5
Distance:	149km
Height gain:	1,998m
Duration:	7 to 9 hours
Verdict:	Peerless scenery, very tough hills, good roads and beautiful villages

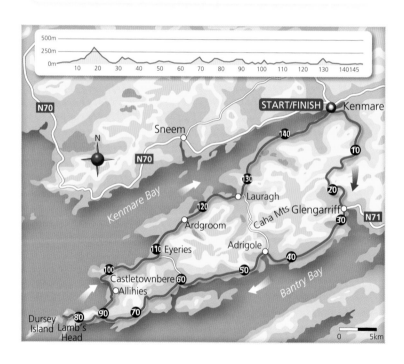

Start/finish

Park to the south of Kenmare, County Kerry. Just before crossing the bridge in the direction of Glengarriff there is a small road to the right. There is plenty of parking space along by the seafront.

The last tunnels on the Kerry side of the Caha Pass en route to Glengarriff, County Cork

This is a tough one, no doubt about it. It has 239m more climbing on a route that is 22km shorter than the Ring of Kerry. It may help to picture it in three stages: first is Kenmare to Glengarriff over the Caha Pass – 26km; from there to the tip of the Beara Peninsula is 61km; another 61km takes us back to Kenmare. Easy peasy!

Route description

Saddle up, cross the bridge and go left on the N71. For a main road, the surface here is quite poor, though sections near Molly Gallivan's pub have been improved. There are walking routes in the vicinity of the pub that take in Neolithic constructions, well worth a look on another day.

After the pub, the road climbs for 4km and passes through several tunnels that straddle the Cork/Kerry border. Water drips from the limestone and may land on the unsuspecting cyclist. The descent starts immediately on the other side, and what a descent it is! Bantry Bay sparkles 10km away with Whiddy Island in the centre of the view. Several roads lead off to the right of the N71, going down to farms that miraculously cling to the valley walls. The route twists and turns, with each view ever more spectacular on the way to Glengarriff.

Continuing on the route, from Glengarriff head west (right). One of the first things to watch out for while cycling along the R572 is Garnish Island, if you can spot it through the lush vegetation. Boat trips are available to what is in effect a tropical island, its microclimate supporting many exotic plants. But today is for the road, and diversions, as enticing as they are, are for another day.

Soon the busy road climbs and great views are afforded of Bantry Bay and Whiddy Island – scene of an oil-terminal explosion in 1979 in which fifty people died. With Sugarloaf Mountain on the right, whoosh along to the elongated village of Adrigole. The next section to Castletownbere is a 15km run with great views of Bere Island and Bantry Bay. Two breaks, at least, are merited on this long cycle and the Copper Kettle in Castletownbere's square is a friend of the cyclist, with delectable scones.

The next leg is a 24km stretch to the Dursey Island cable car at Lamb's Head, all the while on the R572. The cable car is the only one in the country and the prospect of crossing in violent weather conditions makes the heart quiver. Reroute for 8km to a junction passed earlier and bear left for the former copper-mining village of Allihies, which seems to be in a contest with the next village of Eyeries for the most colourfully painted houses.

The scenery hereabouts is glorious and several tough climbs will test the strongest cyclist. Press on to that exotically plumed bird of Eyeries and take a second break in the art-crammed Rhonwen's Bistro, which has a seemingly permanent exhibition of the primitive artist Michael Sheehan, among several other notable artists.

The hardest part of this cycle is now finished and while there are still 40km to go, there are no major hills and the roads are largely good. Next, after a mighty 5km, is the village of Ardgroom, followed 11km later by Lauragh (two nice pubs) and a final 22km run, much of it downhill, to Kenmare Bridge and the car. Bravo!

Taking a rest on the road between Allihies and Eyeries on the Beara Peninsula

46. Dingle Peninsula Circuit

Camp – Anascaul (near) – Dingle – Ventry – Slea Head –
Ballyferriter – Feohanagh – Dingle – Conor Pass – Camp

Location:	County Kerry
Grade:	5
Distance:	126km
Height gain:	1,631m
Duration:	6.5 to 7.5 hours
Verdict:	Outstanding coastal route dodging in and out of mountainsides on a mix of super and poor roads

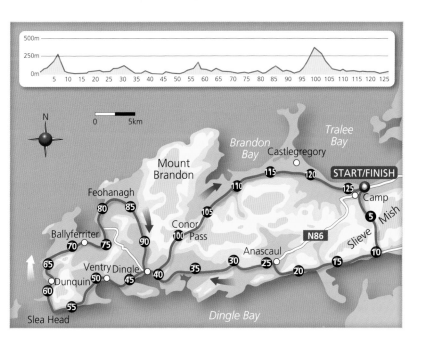

Start/finish

Camp, 15km west of Tralee. Park beside the main road, the N86, at the Camp signpost.

Descending to Castlemaine Harbour, County Kerry

The Iveragh Peninsula would appear to get all the glory with its annual charity ride in which over 10,000 riders take part. However, its northern neighbour is just as alluring. It has its own charming towns and villages, its own group of islands to match the Skelligs of Iveragh. In fact, the Blasket archipelago off Slea Head is arguably as impressive.

The direction of this route is determined by one of Ireland's biggest mountains: Mount Brandon, 953m, lies towards the end of the peninsula and as no road circles its massive flank it is necessary to cross the peninsula twice in order to circumnavigate the mountain. It has just under 100m of ascent less than the 1,759m of the Ring of Kerry cycle on a route that is 45km shorter. It is vital to get the highest point out of the way first, and hence the chosen start point is Camp, some 15km west of Tralee.

Route description

Cycle to the village of Camp 500m further along on the road, to the left. Turn left directly after the church and start the ascent to the highest point at 258m. It is reached after only 6.5km, which indicates a very steep climb, especially towards the end. The views are wonderful, back towards Tralee Bay and with Kerry Head in the distance, while all around are the indomitable mountains whose folds contain the fossils of Silurian trilobites 420 million years old (according to the very informative noticeboard from the Heritage Council).

Now swoop down on Castlemine Harbour like a falcon chasing prey. The road is pretty bad and in some places the ground falls away, making it feel like cycling over a causeway. Continue down to the main road and turn right on the R561. The next node is Anascaul, 7km away. This is a fantastic road with the Atlantic for company, though the traffic makes it a little annoying.

Anascaul is the birthplace of the mighty Tom Crean, polar expeditioner with Shackleton in the early years of the twentieth century. Suitably chastened by his exploits, continue on this puny 126km test. Dingle looms ahead soon and is a good place for a coffee break. The always-lively town has been boosted in recent years by a resident dolphin.

Having completed phase one of three, embark now on the middle section: a 60km circuit around some of the most stunning scenery in the country, returning to Dingle. Take the R559 west to Ventry and press on to Slea Head. All the while the road curves in and out of the mountainside, giving a more remarkable view at each bend. Cruise around the end of the peninsula with the Blasket Islands on the left. Advance to the village of Ballyferriter and on to Feohanagh. This is the famous Slea Head Drive, which is also popular with bikers and tour buses. The road is poor in several places but the views are a great compensation.

Back in Dingle, it is time for another coffee break before the ascent of the mighty Conor Pass, 8km distant. An excellent road eventually leads to the pass at 374m. This is regarded as one of the toughest climbs in the country with a gradient of 8 per cent. Suitably rested and appreciative of the awesome views, roll on down the hill. The car awaits after 25km of descent and some cycling on the flat. Mind-blowing!

47. Mizen Peninsula Circuit

Bantry – Ballydehob – Schull – Toormore – Crookhaven –
Barleycove – Mizen Head – Barleycove – Durrus – Bantry

Location:	County Cork
Grade:	5
Distance:	106km
Height gain:	1,347m
Duration:	6 to 7.5 hours
Verdict:	Cycling with outstanding sea views, salty air and a mix of excellent and poor roads

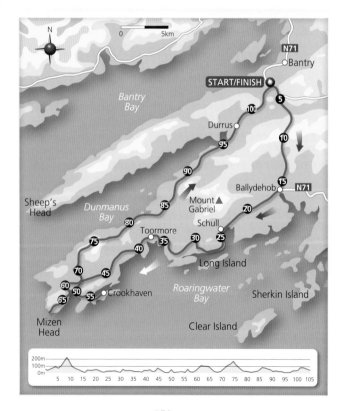

Start/finish

Start point is the Westlodge Hotel, Bantry, on the N71.

Ballydehob Viaduct, County Cork

The Mizen Head may not have the grandeur of the Iveragh Peninsula or the magnificent mountains of the Dingle Peninsula, but what it lacks in earthly glories or natural wonders it makes up for with a simple majesty.

Route description

Head directly south towards Ballydehob. The road to Skibbereen, the R586, continues on straight but the road you need, the N71, cuts off to the right. This is a narrow road though it is well surfaced and you can build up a good speed before a climb to the col at Barnaghgeehy. The wonderfully named Mount Kid is to the left. A superb downhill chase brings you to the lovely village of Ballydehob and its twelve-arch viaduct. Ballydehob has found itself settled by a number of artists and writers attracted by its beautiful setting and excellent pubs.

Continue along on the R592 heading west and, on the right, pass Mount Gabriel with its white meteorological domes. Next comes Schull, 6km farther along. This is another lovely village with a lot to offer the visitor, not least a great bookshop and some choice delicatessens. In its attractive harbour yachts gleam. Leave the main road here by sticking to the coast road, left, in the direction of Colla Pier. A lovely section of the route follows, with low-lying Long Island visible across the waves. The road rises and falls gently amid some spectacular scenery. At Toormore you can almost touch the sea. You pick up the R591 here to the old-world village of Goleen.

Press on to charming Crookhaven, which is, as the name suggests, a crook off the road. Continue on to the amazing beach of Barleycove, formed by the tsunami which resulted from the 1755 earthquake in Lisbon.

One last push from here, cycling above Barleycove, brings you to the tip – Mizen Head itself, where a bridge leads to the old lighthouse, now a visitor centre. No better stop for a break.

About-turn and pick up the road for the north of the peninsula after 5km at the end of the lake. Swing left and snake through the furze bushes for a while before emerging to glorious views of Dunmanus Bay. From here back to Durrus 24km away there are no further hamlets or villages: suffice it to say, the route is not unattractive. From Durrus it is 7km back to base on a fine road, the R591.